CLIMBING
PRAYER
MOUNTAIN

CLIMBING
PRAYER
MOUNTAIN

A 40 DAY PRAYER
JOURNEY INTO THE
PRESENCE OF GOD

TIM SPYKSTRA

Mill Street Press

© 2017 MILL STREET PRESS
SAN LUIS OBISPO, CA

CLIMBING
PRAYER
MOUNTAIN

Published by Mill Street Press
P.O. Box 432
San Luis Obispo, CA 93406

ISBN 978-0-9990722-0-2

Climbing Prayer Mountain may be purchased in bulk for educational, ministry, small groups, business, fund-raising, or sales promotional use. *For information, please e-mail:* ClimbingMaterials@millstreetpress.com

CONTENTS

Climbing with Moses

Climbing with Elijah

Climbing with Jesus

Climbing with Peter & John

FOREWORD

I vividly remember Tim Spykstra telling me the story of how the contents of this book were given to him. It was a Monday. Tim called and said he had spent time earlier that day crying out to God in prayer. The Lord had answered by providing him with the entire concept and outline for this forty-day devotional. Tim even sent me a document containing the topics and scripture passages for each of the forty days. He said it would be titled *"Climbing Prayer Mountain"*. All I could say was, "Wow!"

The irony of the story is that I had just returned home to southern California the night before, after having spent the weekend in Colorado with Tim and his family. I had gone to Denver to accompany Tim into Cañon City Prison and observe his two-day seminar for prisoner/seminary students based upon his book, *The Journey to the Father's Heart*. Unfortunately, we never made it to Cañon City.

At 8:30 pm on Friday evening, Tim's phone rang and we found out that the Cañon City prison was on lockdown for the weekend. We would not be allowed to enter the prison the following day. I'll admit I was relieved, as I was a bit nervous about spending the weekend at the prison. But the look on Tim's face told me that he was devastated. He had been eagerly anticipating this time of ministry with the inmates in Cañon City.

With the seminar canceled, Tim and I had time to fill before my flight home, so we decided to dream into ideas for Oceans Ministries. It was a pleasant weekend, and many topics were touched-upon during our time together, but they remained in the idea stage. I left Denver with mixed feelings–we had not accomplished what we'd originally planned, yet intriguing new ideas were taking shape.

When I received Tim's phone call that Monday, having just returned from spending two somewhat unproductive days together, it was clear to me that the Lord had provided this book to Tim. In his disappointment of having the seminar at Cañon City canceled, Tim had asked God, "*Why?*" This devotional is seemingly God's response to that question.

I know that at the core of Tim Spykstra's heart is a desire to teach people how to have a relationship with the living God. More than that, Tim's desire is for you to experience first-hand the amazing blessings of such a relationship. This devotional provides you with a tool for that purpose. As you read through it, I pray that you will hear what the Lord has intended for you to hear.

– *Henry Miersma*

PREFACE

Climbing Prayer Mountain is a forty-day prayer journey into the presence of God. It is a devotional designed to encourage you in your prayer life and help you grow in fellowship with your Heavenly Father through prayer. My hope is that, through this book, you will experience the presence of your Father, the renewal of His love, and the leading of His Spirit. I'm excited to share this book with you as there is no doubt in my mind that the concept, title, and content for this devotional came from the Lord. Allow me to explain.

Not long ago my wife, Patty, and I spent a summer morning hiking to a well-known mountain lake. Arriving at the destination with aching legs and hearts pounding we took a break to eat our lunches and discussed turning around to head back down the mountain. Just then, a family bounded down towards us from an unmarked trail. When we asked them whether it was worth continuing the hike up the mountain, the father of the family displayed a huge grin and described what was around the bend as **"ridiculously beautiful!"** He encouraged us to go on and promised that we would not be disappointed. Inspired by his words, we ventured ahead and enjoyed one of the most breathtaking hikes we'd ever experienced. I cannot find the words to adequately explain the beauty of the scenery on that mountain. It was unbelievable. Though I had never heard the word combination **"ridiculously beautiful"** before, I decided then that it worked.

Weeks later, I found myself contemplating that word combination again as I studied a familiar section of scripture. I had been in a season of disappointment and discouragement, asking "Why questions" to my Good Father and failing to hear His answer. I plodded forward in my pain, shedding tears and seeking answers from His presence. However, heaven seemed silent. It was then that I opened my Bible to Mark 9 and read the story of Jesus' climb up Mount Hermon with Peter, James, and John.

Jesus knew the amazing cathedral of creation called Mt. Hermon would be an incredible place to commune with His Father. I envisioned myself sitting there with Him at 9,000 feet looking down over the lush landscape of Caesarea Philippi. In my imagination it was awesome. But what happened next would be more awe-inspiring than any words could describe. The glory of heaven exploded out of Jesus: "His clothes became dazzling white, whiter than anyone in the world could bleach them. And there appeared before them Elijah and Moses, who were conversing with Jesus," (vs. 2-3). It must have been **"ridiculously beautiful."**

Later, I pondered why the Father sent Elijah and Moses to join Jesus and a few followers on Mount Hermon. I studied the history of those present on the mountain that day, and my thoughts went to each individual and their specific journey of spiritual growth through prayer. Each one of them learned to pray and climb their own "Prayer Mountain" in order to fellowship with the glorious Heavenly Father. For each, the result was the renewal of the Father's love and the leading of His Spirit.

The voice of the Father began to shake my own soul as I processed the implications of the text. I picked up my laptop and typed several truths from the lives of Moses, Elijah, Jesus, and the disciples who witnessed this **"ridiculously beautiful"** scene. After a few minutes of pounding away on the keyboard, I found my heart quickened by the Father's love–perhaps just like Jesus and the disciples experienced as they were engulfed in the glory cloud and heard, *"This is my Son, whom I love. Listen to Him!"* (vs. 7). I sensed the Father say to me "Climb Prayer Mountain with my Son Jesus, along with Moses, Elijah, Peter, James, and John. Let them lead you up into the Heavenly Prayer Mountain to experience my glorious love for you. Share these prayer truths with others!" This book is the result and encompasses a few of the many lessons gleamed from these spiritual mountain climbers.

In addition to studying Biblical texts, a survey on prayer was sent out to people who read my weekly blog. I was overwhelmed by the responses received. Included were comments from those who felt guilty for not praying enough, to questions about how to hear God's voice. Also gleaned from the questionnaire were references to the battle that many face in their prayer life against busyness. I feel compelled to address this question directly, as the reason for this inner struggle for intimate time with our Father is why this book was written. The enemy knows that communing with the Father is the most important spiritual exercise one can do. Therefore, he will place boulders and slithery snakes along the trail to hinder your climb. Spiritual storms, battles with self-doubt, extreme guilt, and struggles with indwelling sin may come out of nowhere at times. Yes, Satan will do whatever he can to keep you from *"Climbing Prayer Mountain."*

But don't give in to his wicked schemes. Keep pressing upward. Remember, you aren't alone–the Father has given you the Holy Spirit as a partner for the journey. Tap into the Holy Spirit; He will give you daily strength and fortitude. The Holy Spirit will be your teacher, revealing the truths from Jesus, Moses, Elijah, and the disciples. When you do stumble or fall, He will be there to pick you up. When you don't know how to pray or even what to pray for, be encouraged He prays for you:

"...the Spirit helps us in our weakness. We do not know what we ought to pray for, but the Spirit himself intercedes for us with groans that words cannot express. And He who searches our hearts knows the mind of the Spirit, because the Spirit intercedes for the saints in accordance with God's will." Romans 8:26-27

Yes, prayer can be a hard spiritual hike: your spiritual muscles will ache, doubts will pound inside your head like a severe headache, and you may even feel a dehydration of the soul. At times you will want to quit and head back down to a more comfortable, safe place. But the reason to keep climbing is because the journey will ultimately lead you to a place that is unbelievably beautiful.

As you take on this challenge to climb *Prayer Mountain* over the next 40 days, I pray that you will experience the presence of your Father. I pray that you will know the Father's love for you as a river that flows down the mountain. May this river flood your soul! I pray that you, too, would use the words **"ridiculously beautiful"** to describe the Father and His love for you!

– *Tim Spykstra*

USING THE DAILY MATERIALS

Each of the forty days contains a devotional in which Tim Spykstra draws truths from both his own personal experiences as well as pivotal events in the spiritual growth of either Moses, Elijah, Jesus, or Peter & John. As you read the devotionals, consider how to apply the truths found within them to your own life.

In addition, each day also contains a scripture passage for you to ponder, meditate on and pray into. Ponder the passage by reading it several times, then pray into it using the prayer prompts as a starting point. Ask the Holy Spirit to guide your prayers as you journey into the presence of God.

USING THE STUDY QUESTIONS

A series of questions provided for extended study are located at the end of each ten-day section. You may choose to use the questions daily during a forty-day study, or within an eight-week group study setting (questions are organized for the latter). In either case, using a journal is encouraged. Page references are included at the end of each day providing the location for that day's questions. Questions are numbered using a #.# system where the first number refers to the day the question is drawn from. For example, question 2.3 is the third question drawn from day number two.

Out of a wilderness experience, God drew Moses to himself and revealed Himself to him. God wants that same type of relationship with you.

CLIMBING WITH
MOSES

*God draws us into
a relationship
with Himself
through prayer.*

Day 1

FINDING THE MOUNTAIN

Now Moses was tending the flock of Jethro…
and he led the flock to the far side of the desert
and came to Horeb, the mountain of God.
– EXODUS 3:1

The story of Moses is a great example of finding *Prayer Mountain*. Not the physical act of finding God in the burning bush on Mount Horeb, but rather, the spiritual act of meeting a Holy God and developing a relationship with Him through prayer. It may appear that Moses found God's mountain by accident while searching for grass for his hungry sheep. But as is the case for everyone who finds *Prayer Mountain*, it was the mountain–God Himself–who found Moses, and it was not an accident.

God called Moses to this mountain before he was born. His plan was that Moses would come to intimately know Him and follow after Him, just as sheep journey in the footsteps of their shepherd. Moses' destiny was to be God's shepherd staff used to lead Israel out of 400 years of slavery in Egypt, back home to the land of promise.

But before Moses could fulfill his destiny, he had to learn humility. He had to learn that the privilege and position he held as a member of Pharaoh's house did not qualify him to decide how, or when, the Israelites would be freed from slavery. Moses' lesson came as a result of his impetuous act of killing an Egyptian guard. Because he took matters into his own hands, he lost both his privileged status in Egypt and the respect of his fellow Israelites. Without a people to call his own, Moses fled Egypt to endure several decades of isolation in the desert.

Standing before the burning bush at the age of eighty, Moses' heart had been marinated by isolation and insignificance for forty years. His heart had been prepared in the hot, humbling furnace of the desert for the refreshing river of grace that would flow from the Mountain of God.

I was led to *Prayer Mountain* at an early age because of difficult circumstances at home. As I look back to those days, a time where my only solace came when kneeling at my bed crying out to God, I now see it was a divine set-up. The Father used my pain and isolation to prepare me for His presence.

Where are you on your spiritual journey? Maybe your journey is like mine, where difficult situations have sent you repeatedly to your knees. Or maybe you can relate to Moses, having tried to handle life through your own resources, only to wake up one day to find yourself in a spiritual wasteland. It is also possible that, like the younger version of Moses, you're still trying to live life on your own terms.

After years of studying the landscape of prayer and those who have made the climb up *Prayer Mountain*, I have found that, though everyone's journey will be different, the heart condition will be the same. Our good Father will always use humility to show us our need to begin the climb. Proverbs 3:34 states: *"God opposes the proud but gives grace to the humble."*

Chances are, the reason you picked up this devotional was because a mysterious hand is leading you, like it did Moses, directing you to the one who loves you more than you know. *Prayer Mountain* awaits you, just as it did Moses. My hope is that you, too, will humble yourself, commit to *Climbing Prayer Mountain*, and experience the refreshing river of grace that flows from the Mountain of God.

PONDER | MEDITATE | PRAY

PONDER JAMES 4:7-10

*Submit yourselves, then to God. Resist the devil, and he will
flee from you. Come near to God and He will come near to
you. Wash your hands you sinners, and purify your hearts you
double-minded. Grieve, mourn and wail. Change your laughter
to mourning and your joy to gloom. Humble yourselves before the
Lord, and He will lift you up.*

MEDITATE ON AND PRAY INTO JAMES 4:7-10

Praise God:

– for being the same God to us as He was to Moses

Tell God:

– about the things that take your focus away from Him

Thank God:

– for His mercy

– for His faithfulness

Ask God:

– for humility

– to prepare your heart for a climb

– for the desire to know Him more–to climb Prayer Mountain

– for the discipline to continue Climbing Prayer Mountain

– to speak to your heart

EXTENDED STUDY QUESTIONS: PAGE 58

*The goal of prayer
is an encounter with
the living God,
the "I Am the King
of Everything."*

Day 2

THE KING OF THE MOUNTAIN

God said to Moses, 'I AM WHO I AM.'.

– EXODUS 3:14

My kids and I were filled with anticipation as we climbed our first 14,000-foot mountain in the rugged Colorado Rockies. Halfway up we were confronted with a group of hikers hurrying down; they strongly encouraged us to turn back as a thunderstorm was approaching quickly. In hindsight we were probably crazy, but we continued up the trail and found an old wooden shelter to wait out the storm. After about twenty minutes of mountain-shaking wind and pelting rain there was a breakthrough, at which point a glorious rainbow appeared leading us to the summit. The experience was an unforgettable rush in the glory of God's majestic creation.

Moses' glorious encounter with God in Exodus 3 was preceded by a storm that lasted not twenty minutes, but forty years. Humbled by the storms of life and never-ending days in solitude chasing sheep up, down, and around the wilderness and mountains, he was now ready to meet the LORD of the mountain.

God chose to introduce Himself to Moses in a bush that would not burn up. As you approach *Prayer Mountain*, you will find that your Good Father will meet you in the strangest ways to grab your full attention. The God who made you knows just how to communicate with you. For Moses, it was through a fiery bush.

As Moses inched toward this glorious sight, a voice came from the bush saying: *"Take off your sandals, for the place where you are standing is holy ground… I am the God of your Father Abraham, the God of Isaac and the God of Jacob,"* (3:4-6). This encounter rocked Moses with fear, and although he had to look away, he continued listening. He heard God tell of His grace-filled plan to liberate His children from the prison of Egypt and bring them into a land filled with glorious promises of freedom. He also heard God say He had chosen him, Moses, to lead His people out of Egypt.

These words pricked at Moses' deep insecurities. Flooded with fear he cried out to God, *"Who am I...?"* (vs. 11). Moses was sure God had picked the wrong guy–you and I would probably do the same–but God reassured him by promising He would go with him.

God then offers one of the greatest revelations in Scripture–His name. It was the name Moses was to share with the children of Israel, ***"I AM WHO I AM"*** (vs. 14), the Hebrew word YHVH. There are numerous ways to capture the meaning of this name, but I like to translate it "I AM The King of Everything!"

Our goal in *Climbing Prayer Mountain* is an encounter with the living God, the same "I AM The King of Everything!" that Moses met on Mt. Horeb. For Moses, this encounter transformed him from a broken shepherd into a mighty warrior held by the protective hands of the Great I AM.

For you and me, transformation is also possible. Our task is to keep climbing *Prayer Mountain* and not allow life's storms to turn us back. Through prayer, we can learn to listen for God's voice–to look for our "burning bush"–and experience an encounter with Him.

As with Moses, God has a calling on our lives, we just need to be willing to listen and hear it. No matter what that calling is, we can rest in the knowledge that The Great I AM promises to go with us.

PONDER | MEDITATE | PRAY

PONDER REVELATION 1:17-18

When I saw Him, I fell at His feet as though dead. Then He placed His right hand on me and said: 'Do not be afraid. I am the First and the Last. I am the Living One, I was dead, and behold I am alive forever and ever.

MEDITATE ON AND PRAY INTO REVELATION 1:17-18

Praise God:

– for being YHVH - the "I AM The King of Everything!"

Tell God:

– about the things that make it hard for you to hear Him

Thank God:

– for appearing to Moses in the burning bush

– for His promise to go with you

Ask God:

– for humility

– to reveal Himself to you

– for the discipline to climb Prayer Mountain

– to speak to your heart

EXTENDED STUDY QUESTIONS: PAGE 58

Place your trust in the mighty hands of God.

Day 3

MOVING THE MIGHTY HAND OF GOD

Then the LORD said to Moses, "Now you will see what I will do to Pharaoh: Because of my mighty hand he will let them go; because of my mighty hand he will drive them out of his country."

– EXODUS 6:1-2

Early in my football-playing days, while still in grade school, I was physically too small to grip the football. As a result, I couldn't control my throws. Regardless, my coach tried playing me at quarterback and even sprayed my hands with sticky stuff to help me throw the football. Needless to say, I was moved to another position shortly after that.

Perhaps God gave me small hands to daily remind me that I'm not in control, so that I would lift those hands up in prayer and cry, "Help." At a young age, God brought me to my knees because of impossible situations that my little heart and hands could not handle. He was teaching me early-on to trust in the mighty hands of Father God who could lift any mountain of difficulty I faced.

Moses and the children of Israel encountered an impossible situation in the form of the cruelty imposed upon them by Pharaoh, which kept their lives in constant chaos. Yet Pharaoh and his hellish hordes would prove to be no match for the hand of God that would be released by the prayer groans of His people and the passionate plea of His servant Moses. In Exodus 6, Moses cries out, *"O Lord, why have you brought trouble upon this people? Is this why you sent me?"* (Ex. 5:22). Notice how God handles Moses' troubled heart: He responds, *"Now you will see what I will do to Pharaoh: Because of my mighty hand he will let them go..."* (Ex. 6:1).

On this journey up *Prayer Mountain*, don't miss the opportunity to bring your impossible situations and place them in the compassionate, mighty hands of our Father. In day two, we learned He is the Great "I AM" who is "The King of Everything!" In Exodus 6:6-8, the Lord responds to Moses and the people with promises from His *mighty hand*. These promises belong to you and me when we call on Him in prayer. They are:

- I will free you from the bondage of your enemies, sins, and addictions.

- I will redeem you through the blood of the Lamb, through my son, Jesus, who forgives all your sins.

- I will take you as my beloved children, and I will be your loving Father.

- I will bring you into my perfect promises for you, just as I promised to your parents with uplifted hand, and you will possess my Kingdom.

Each promise starts with the words *I will.* Prayer enables us to place our life into the Father's hands, and He promises to hear and act because of His great love for us.

Later in chapter 6, the people of Israel struggle to believe in a God who would make true on His promises. Yet in spite of their doubts, the Father moves forward out of love for His children. What a God, one who acts even when His children struggle to trust! Today, once again bring your impossibilities and place them in **His Mighty Hands**.

PONDER | MEDITATE | PRAY

PONDER ISAIAH 41:10

So do not fear, for I am with you, do not be dismayed, for I am your God. I will strengthen you and help you; I will uphold you with my righteous right hand.

MEDITATE ON AND PRAY INTO ISAIAH 41:10

Praise God:

– for being a God who can handle the impossible

Tell God:

– about your impossible situations

Thank God:

– for keeping His promises

Ask God:

– to support you with His mighty hand, to strengthen you

– to reveal Himself to you

– to speak to your heart

❖ EXTENDED STUDY QUESTIONS: PAGE 59

Learn how to be still.

Day 4

WHEN YOU'RE BETWEEN THE DEVIL AND THE DEEP BLUE SEA

The Lord will fight for you; you only need to be still.

– EXODUS 14:14

One of the most recorded events in biblical history is the crossing of the Red Sea by the children of Israel. In a sense, the Israelites were "born again" as their life of slavery to Pharaoh was replaced by freedom. They became sons and daughters of the King of Kings as they crossed the sea on dry ground and then witnessed the demise of Pharaoh and his army beneath its crashing waves.

Think about the events leading up to this astonishing moment. After the Passover concluded in death for all firstborn sons who did not have blood smeared above their home's doorframe, Pharaoh practically chased the Israelites away. Then Pharaoh changed his mind again. He began pursuing the Israelites across the Egyptian desert with his armies hell-bent on revenge.

Just when it looked as if release from bondage was a reality for the Israelites, they found themselves in a heartbreaking trap. Pharaoh and his armies were quickly approaching from behind them. An uncrossable body of water, the Red Sea, lay before them. It is within this historic biblical drama we find a crucial prayer point for *Climbing Prayer Mountain*.

What do you do when you're between the devil and the deep blue sea? Or in the Israelites' case, Pharaoh and the deep Red Sea? You cry to God for help! Not only did Israel do this, but they also flooded their leader, Moses, with a series of complaints, blaming him for their awful predicament (Ex. 14:10-12).

But give Moses credit, he had learned a thing or two about God on his own *Prayer Mountain*. He calmly responded to the frantic people: "*Do not be afraid. Stand firm and you will see the deliverance the LORD will bring you today. The Egyptians you see today, you will never see again. The LORD will fight for you; you need only to be still.*" Exodus 13-14.

Reread the last part of vs. 14, *"You need only to be still."* This is an all important prayer point! Dead-ends and roadblocks will come, but it is essential for us to learn how to respond. When we face a ferocious enemy and no escape is apparent, **"Be still!"**

The word **still** means to quiet yourself, not by looking back at the enemy or at the sea of impossibility before you, but rather by looking up to the LORD, the One who "fights for you." The Father will not abandon you in your trial.

Over the years, the Spirit has taught me that one of the most powerful prayers I can pray is one to quiet my fearful mind. I can sometimes get consumed with what is behind and before me, so I have learned to take deep breaths and look up at the Revelation 5 Jesus who is reigning right now as the Lion and the Lamb King. *He is the one who controls the unfolding of history.* The more I breathe in King Jesus and sit in silence mediating on His glorious reign, the more His life-giving peace pushes out fear and panic. Ah, that is where I desire to live!

Be still prayers are desperately needed in a culture consumed with nonstop rushing, rooted in the fear of what is behind and before. At this moment, take a few deep breaths and still your rushing mind. Just gaze on King Jesus, your deliverer.

PONDER | MEDITATE | PRAY

PONDER PSALM 46:10-11

Be still and know that I am God. I will be exalted among the nations; I will be exalted in the earth. The Lord Almighty is with us; the God of Jacob is our fortress.

MEDITATE ON AND PRAY INTO PSALM 46:10-11

Praise God:

– for being a God who can part the Red Sea

– for being one who controls the unfolding of history

Tell God:

– about your "pharaohs" and your "blue seas"

Thank God:

– for the promise of deliverance

Ask God:

– to help you quiet your spirit

– to provide His peace

❖ EXTENDED STUDY QUESTIONS: PAGES 59-60

*Gratitude is essential
in our prayer life.*

Day 5

PLAY YOUR TAMBOURINE

I will sing to the LORD for He is highly exalted.
The horse and its rider He has hurled into the sea.

– EXODUS 15:1

One time when leaving a church I pastored, I received a parting gift of a tambourine from a young man named Michael. Michael and his family would sit in the middle of the sanctuary, and I always knew he was in church when I heard him play his tambourine during worship. I would smile to myself in the front row, hearing him play his rhythmic beat with a joyful boldness. His worship would push me out of my comfort zone into a deeper celebration for the gift of salvation freely given to me in Jesus Christ. As Michael handed me the gift, he said; "Now, Pastor Tim, I want you to play your own tambourine!"

In Exodus 15, Moses and his sister, Miriam, sing, shake the tambourine, and dance before the Lord. It is their response to their salvation from bondage in Egypt and the destruction of Pharaoh and his army in the Red Sea. Moses teaches us that *Prayer Mountain* is a place saturated with praise and worship. One of the greatest ways to open up the heavens and experience the presence of God is to sing, dance, shout, or play whatever instrument you are able; joyfully praising God for His gift of salvation, given to you through His Son.

Can you imagine what the worship time was like on the shoreline of the Red Sea? These former slaves in bondage to a cruel taskmaster, released by a divine intervention, are now free as sons and daughters to skip into the promises of God. Picture the dancing, tambourine playing, and singing. The paraphrased words from Exodus 15:1-18 are sung out of a heart of great gratitude:

The LORD is my strength and my song; He has become my salvation. He is my God and I will praise Him, my father's God, and I will exalt Him...Who is like you – majestic in holiness, awesome in glory, working wonders? You stretched out your right hand and the earth swallowed them. In your unfailing love you will lead the people you have redeemed... You will bring them in and plant them on the mountain of your inheritance, the place, O LORD, you made for your dwelling...The Lord will reign forever and ever.

This is the first recorded corporate worship time found in the scriptures, and it illustrates the pattern of praise that should take place on our *Prayer Mountain.* We are to be children who bring unhindered worship before a Father God who has poured out His *unfailing love* to us in Jesus. We are no longer slaves to sin, but we are children of the King, sealed with the Holy Spirit's power to live in freedom. We are free to dance, free to sing, and free to shout the glory of our risen King!

I doubt that many of you own a tambourine, but I hope you understand my point. Whether you sing, dance, play an instrument, or worship and praise God quietly with unabashed joy in your heart, God deserves unhindered gratitude and utmost praise. Join the throngs of the redeemed in offering up heartfelt worship to your good, good Father.

PONDER | MEDITATE | PRAY

PONDER PSALM 100

Shout for joy to the LORD, all the earth. Worship the LORD with gladness; come before Him with joyful songs. Know that the LORD is God. It is He who made us, and we are His; we are His people the sheep of His pasture. Enter His gates with thanksgiving and His courts with praise; give thanks to Him and praise His name. For the LORD is good and His love endures forever; His faithfulness continues through all generations.

MEDITATE ON AND PRAY INTO PSALM 100

Praise God:

– for who He is

– for what He has done for you

– for His faithfulness

Tell God:

– about your struggles with sin

Thank God:

– for His mercy

Ask God:

– to help you bring unhindered praise

– to provide His joy

❖ EXTENDED STUDY QUESTIONS: PAGE 60

❖

Instead of becoming bitter, pray.

❖

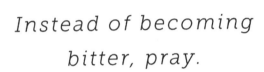

Day 6

TURNING THE BITTER INTO A BLESSING

Then Moses cried out to the LORD, and the LORD showed him a piece of wood. He threw it into the water, and the water became sweet.

– EXODUS 15:25

Grumbling is our national pastime. If you don't believe me take a quick look at social media. There you'll find angry rants about the president, the performance of a favorite team, hot weather, cold weather, an ex-lover, the price of a cup of coffee–the list is endless. I tend to join the grumblers when the car breaks down or when sitting in Denver traffic and my all-important schedule is altered. Complaining just seems to be part of our flawed DNA.

So we have to take it easy on the Israelites when, a few days after the miracle at the Red Sea, they are grumbling about the heat and lack of water to quench their thirst. When they finally found a drinking hole at Marah, the water was bitter and undrinkable.

I'm sure I would have joined in with their accosting of Moses for their bleak circumstance. It was the last straw. With parched mouths, looking at a pool of water they could not drink, they yelled to Moses, "What are we to drink?"

The amazing thing is how Moses responded. Instead of yelling back, which I might have done, it says, *"Moses cried out to the LORD..."* (Ex. 15:25). He took the bitter situation and brought it right to the LORD. Think, if we did this first when we face bitter waters, what a difference it would make! For one thing, our blood pressure would fall back to normal, and a peace might replace our anxiety.

We can tell God is pleased with Moses' response to the situation, as He immediately reveals the solution to Moses. God shows Moses a piece of wood to be thrown into the water, which transforms the bitter water into sweet refreshment. God uses this episode of Moses' prayer and the altering of the waters to teach us a deep truth about the power of prayer vs. the spirit of unbelief seen in grumbling.

Here is what the LORD communicates to His people in Exodus 15:26. *"If you listen carefully to the voice of the LORD your God and do what is right in His eyes, if you pay attention to His command and keep all His decrees, I will not bring on you any of the diseases I brought on the Egyptians, for I am the LORD, who heals you."*

Yes, life is going to bring about bitter times. But the LORD calls us, His people, to bring our bitterness to Him, just as Moses did in his prayer at Marah. By doing so, we announce our dependence on our Sovereign God and place our trust in Him to take the bitter and turn it into a blessing.

Moses encountered the LORD, the I AM, on the mountain and experienced His healing hand restoring him to his true calling. Moses had learned over many years that a grumbling spirit brings about a life infested with bitterness and leaves one spiritually thirsty. Healing can only flow from the rivers of heaven's love, accessed by crying out to the Father for help.

So the next time you feel a grumbling spirit begin to surface and you're ready to spew anger out of your heart, stop for a moment. Instead, cry-out to your Father for help. Place your trust in Him. Allow His healing waters to flow your way.

PONDER | MEDITATE | PRAY

PONDER PSALM 40:1-3

I waited patiently for the LORD; He turned to me and heard my cry. He lifted me out of the slimy pit out of the mud and mire; He set my feet on a rock and gave me a firm place to stand. He put a new song in my mouth, a hymn of praise to our God. Many will see and fear and put their trust in the LORD.

MEDITATE ON AND PRAY INTO PSALM 40:1-3

Praise God:

– for His ability to change the bitter into a blessing

– for being trustworthy

Tell God:

– what makes you bitter

Thank God:

– for blessings received

Ask God:

– to help you change your bitterness into blessing

– to send His healing waters

EXTENDED STUDY QUESTIONS: PAGE 61

*It is a
privilege to
pray for others.*

Day 7

OPENING HEAVEN FOR OTHERS

But Moses sought the favor of the LORD his God. 'O LORD,' he said,
'Why should your anger burn against your people, whom you
brought out of Egypt with great power and a mighty hand?'
– EXODUS 32:11

One vital truth God taught me at a young age was the privilege and the power of praying for others. For over 10 years, I daily knelt at my bed and cried out to God on behalf of my father. He was in a horrific battle with alcohol and nothing was releasing him from this demonic stronghold. I loved my dad and begged God to free him from the grip of alcohol.

There were times I faced discouragement as things kept spiraling downward, yet the Spirit continued to prompt me to pray and not give up hope. After over 3,650 prayers, heaven opened, and the healing power of God the Father liberated my father. This miracle, birthed in prayer, transformed my prayer life and forever roused within me a desire to intercede for others.

If you make a list of fervent interceders in the Bible, Moses would be near the top. Throughout the story of the Exodus, it is apparent Moses' greatest work was bringing people into the presence of God through prayer. It is amazing to note that many of those he lifts up are those who beat him down. Look at these examples of people Moses prayed for:

- For Pharaoh. After Pharaoh is overwhelmed by the plagues, he asks Moses to pray to the LORD for relief (Ex. 8:8, 28; 9:28; 10:17).

- For his sister, Miriam, who opposed him and was struck with leprosy (Num. 12:13).

- For the Israelites, after their sin of worshiping the golden calf (Ex. 32:30-32).

- For the Israelites, after the rebellion of Korah and 250 other leaders who opposed Moses' leadership (Num. 16:22).

- For the Israelites, after they were in opposition to Moses and Aaron because they lacked water (Num. 20:6).

- For healing from the attack of the venomous snakes upon those who complained against God (Num. 21:7).

- For the Israelites, after they believed the ten spies who said it would be impossible to enter the promised land (Num. 14:13-19).

God the Father answered every prayer in this list with a "Yes". In fact, all of Moses' prayers of intercession were motivated out of a love and a desire for the glory of God. When you pray for others out of a heart of love and a desire to see God's holy name worshiped, your prayers will find a home before the throne of the King of glory, and He will act.

What a wonderful privilege we've been given to pray for others, yes, even those who may oppose us, and to ask God to move on their behalf. Your prayers can change the destiny of countless people in our world. Don't hesitate to open the doors of heaven for someone in need!

PONDER | MEDITATE | PRAY

PONDER 1 TIMOTHY 2:1

I urge, then, first of all, that requests, prayers, intercession and thanksgiving be made for everyone.

MEDITATE ON AND PRAY INTO 1 TIMOTHY 2:1

Ask God:

– to give you His eyes and show you people to pray for

Tell God:

– about the people in your life who need help

Thank God:

- for answering your prayers

Ask God:

- to help those people He's given you to pray for

❖ EXTENDED STUDY QUESTIONS: PAGE 61

Being in God's presence will spur you to want more of God's presence.

Day 8

THE CRY OF YOUR HEART

Then Moses said, 'Now show me your glory.'
– EXODUS 33:18

What is the deepest longing of your heart? Stop reading for a moment and take some time to honestly reflect and wrestle with that question. I would love to sit with you at a local coffee shop and hear your response. If I were to sit with Moses at a coffee shop and chat with him concerning the inquiry, I'm 100% sure his passionate response would be "*the presence of my LORD.*"

Moses gives his answer away in one of my favorite passages in God's Word, Exodus 33:12-23. The context of this passage is a pointed conversation between Moses and God concerning Israel and who will lead them to the Promised Land. Because of their worship of the golden calf, God told Moses He would send an angel to lead them instead of His holy presence.

Moses fervently says to God, "*If your Presence does not go with us, do not send us up from here,*" (vs. 15). The problem for Moses stems back to his encounter with the Great "I AM" in the burning bush. Moses had been "ruined" by the Presence of God. Once you taste His Presence, you can't live without it.

Throughout Scripture, men and women who entered into the throne room of God's Glory would forever desire more of God's presence. The Apostle Paul is a great example of this heartfelt desire. Paul was persecuting new believers, but once he saw the resurrected Jesus on the road to Damascus he was a changed man. He developed a burning desire, a thirst for more of Him, that never ceased: "*I want to know Christ and the power of His resurrection...*" (Philippians 3:10).

Even though, *"The LORD would speak to Moses face to face, as a man speaks with his friend,"* (Ex.33:11) Moses asked the LORD for more, *"If you are pleased with me, teach me your ways so I may know you and continue to find favor with you..."* (vs. 13). This is a prayer our Father loves to answer, and He responds by saying: *"My Presence will go with you, and I will give you rest,"* (vs. 15). Later, after God tells Moses He is pleased with him and knows him by name, Moses still wants more. He makes this plea of God: *"Now show me your glory,"* (vs. 18).

A warning: when you climb *Prayer Mountain* and glimpse your Father through prayer, you too will desire more of His Presence and cry out, "Now show me your glory." Every other longing in your heart will pale in comparison to the passion for His Presence.

Your heart was created to commune with your Father, and nothing found on earth will satisfy the void except Him. My prayer for you as you read this devotional is that you would join in the prayer of Moses and cry out to the Father to show you His glory and be forever ruined by His presence. This is the end gain of prayer: dwelling in the Father's presence.

PONDER | MEDITATE | PRAY

PONDER PSALM 27:4

One thing I ask of the LORD, this is what I seek; that I may dwell in the house of the LORD all the days of my life to gaze upon the beauty of the LORD and seek Him in His temple.

MEDITATE ON AND PRAY INTO PSALM 27:4

Praise God:

– for allowing Moses to see His glory

Tell God:

– about the desires of your heart

Thank God:

– for His presence

Ask God:

– to show you His glory

❖ EXTENDED STUDY QUESTIONS: PAGE 62

*God wants you to know
that He loves you.*

Day 9

WHAT THE LORD LOVES TO SAY

> *The LORD, the LORD the compassionate and gracious God,*
> *slow to anger, abounding in love and faithfulness, maintaining love to*
> *thousands, and forgiving wickedness, rebellion and sin.*
> *Yet He does not leave the guilty unpunished;*
> *He punishes the children and their children for*
> *the sin of the fathers to the third and forth generation.*
> – EXODUS 34:6-7

If prayer is a conversation with God, a big portion of our prayer time should be spent listening. When my son TJ was around three years old, he talked incessantly, asking question after question. In fact, I remember debating with my wife over who would sit with TJ for a five hour plane trip, knowing the time would be filled with nonstop inquisitive chatter and no nap!

In God's ears, my early prayer life must have sounded like TJ at three years old. I did all the talking. I peppered God with requests, pleas, and a lot of questions. Over the years I have learned the value of speaking less and listening more to the heart of Father, for what He has to say is life-changing.

After Moses prayed to see the Glory of God, he was told to hang out in a cave and wait for God's presence to pass by. The backside of God's glory and brilliance was all that Moses would be able to handle. Yet, the day did come when God revealed Himself in a radiant glory cloud that covered Moses on the mountain and left Moses' face glowing for days. But it was the words from the Father that day, found in Ex. 34:6-7, which would grab Moses' heart. Holy words that would be repeated forty more times in the Scriptures; words that would eventually come to life in Jesus Christ almost 1,500 years later.

As Moses listened in prayer, he heard from the Father the words, *"I am compassionate and gracious, slow to anger, and abounding in love and faithfulness."* The blessings from God's heart continued flowing, *"maintaining love to thousands, and forgiving wickedness, rebellion and sin."* What good news! The Father desires to share what He is really like with all who listen. And yet, because He is a Holy God, there is judgment upon those who refuse to listen and walk away from His gracious offer of forgiveness and everlasting love.

One of my spiritual disciplines is to read a Psalm each day as well as verses from the Gospels. As I read, I listen for my Father's voice in the life and teachings of His Son Jesus, who is His *"exact representation of His being,"* (Heb. 1:3). Jesus turns the words of Exodus 34:6-7 into living color; they become a powerful source of daily bread. Most days I awake with an eager anticipation to hear what the Father desires to say to me. I find there is never enough time; it always goes way too fast, and He has tons more to say if I would sit, just sit, and listen a little longer.

As Moses found out on the *Mountain*, God is a Good Father wishing to pour out unending love on all who will take the time and listen to what He loves to say. My prayer is that you will take the time to listen daily to the Father.

PONDER | MEDITATE | PRAY

PONDER JEREMIAH 31:3 (THE MESSAGE)

This is the way God put it: 'They found grace out in the desert, these people who survived the killing. Israel, out looking for a place to rest, met God out looking for them.' God told them, 'I've never quit loving you and never will. Expect love, love, and more love!'

MEDITATE ON AND PRAY INTO JEREMIAH 31:3

Praise God:

– for being a God who listens to your prayers

Tell God:

– about your needs, both physical and spiritual

Thank God:

- for His promise to never stop loving you

Ask God:

– to help you to hear what He has to say to you

EXTENDED STUDY QUESTIONS: PAGES 62-63

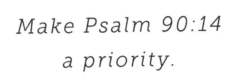

*Make Psalm 90:14
a priority.*

Day 10

FINAL WORDS FROM THE MOUNTAIN

Lord, you have been our dwelling place
throughout all generations. Before the mountains
were born or you brought forth the earth and the world
from everlasting to everlasting you are God.
– PSALM 90:1-2

Psalm 90, written by Moses, is read at many funerals. I've tapped into the beauty of this Psalm myself, quoting vs. 12; *"Teach us to number our days aright that we may gain a heart of wisdom."* Nothing helps put life into right perspective like contemplating one's final day on earth. I like to imagine that Moses wrote this Psalm right before his death, passing these words onto the Joshua generation who were about enter the Promised Land.

Moses was not allowed to enter the Promised Land because of a sin he committed in regards to hitting a rock for water instead of speaking to it as God commanded (Num. 20). So before Moses died, God instructed him to climb Mount Nebo, where He would show him the land promised to his forefathers, the land which was about to be delivered to Israel. At 120 years old, Moses made the trek. No doubt he stood, in bittersweet amazement, gazing over this glorious land and the promise about to be fulfilled.

Moses wrote Psalm 90 as a song for the children to sing, a song from the heart of a seasoned *Prayer Mountain* climber. On his wild ride of faith, Moses had learned what mattered most in life, and in Psalm 90's seventeen verses, he leaves us a lifetime of wisdom to ponder and pray over.

"Lord, you have been our dwelling place..." Even though the Israelites were about to take over the Promised Land and call it their home, in reality their home was in the presence of the LORD. Without His presence, no place on earth could feel like home. According to Moses, we are just like "new grass" that pops-up in the morning and by evening is "dry and withered" and gone (vs. 5).

Many years ago I memorized verse 14, which for me captures the heart of Moses and his desire for a life filled with lasting meaning: *"Satisfy us in the morning with your unfailing love, that we may sing for joy and be glad all our days."*

So before I munch on my bowl of my favorite cereal, I come to my Father and pray for a spoonful of His unfailing love. In Hebrew, *unfailing love* means checed, or His "goodness, kindness, merciful, and overflowing gracious love." This *unfailing love* will bring "joy unspeakable" to my day and spills over to the world around me, so I can reveal to others what my Father looks like.

I challenge you to hide verse 14 in your heart. Recite it every morning when you first awake. Make it your daily passion in prayer, and you will dwell daily on *Prayer Mountain*, where your Father lives.

PONDER | MEDITATE | PRAY

PONDER PSALM 90:14

Satisfy me in the morning with your unfailing love, that I may sing for joy and be glad all our days.

MEDITATE ON AND PRAY INTO PSALM 90:14

Praise God:

– for the example He's given us in the life of Moses

Tell God:

– that you love Him

Thank God:

- for His unfailing love

Ask God:

– to satisfy you with His unfailing love

EXTENDED STUDY QUESTIONS: PAGE 63

CLIMBING WITH
MOSES

QUESTIONS FOR
EXTENDED STUDY

WEEK 1: DAYS 1-5

DAY 1: FINDING THE MOUNTAIN

1.1) Why have you started on this spiritual climb up Prayer Mountain? Do you sense somehow, like Moses, the Spirit of God's hand is leading you to encounter Him in a deeper way through prayer?

1.2) As I shared with you in Day 1, it was at an early age because of difficult circumstances at home, I learned to climb Prayer Mountain. Have you experienced humbling times in your life where you cried out to God in desperation?

1.3) Everyone's journey to Prayer Mountain is unique, yet as I said "the heart condition will be the same." As you think of the first 80 years of Moses' life as described in Exodus 1 & 2, how did God prepare Moses' heart to encounter Him on Mount Sinai?

DAY 2: THE KING OF THE MOUNTAIN

2.1) When Moses' heart was humbled and made ready, God spoke to him on a mountain through a bush that would not burn up (Ex. 3:2). As you look over your life, what are some of the ways God has grabbed your attention and spoken to you?

2.2) At this time read Exodus 3 and as you do try to put yourself in Moses' shoes. What do you think caused him more fear, the presence of God or the fact that God was calling him to do the impossible?

2.3) To calm Moses' fears, God introduces Himself to Moses by name, "I AM WHO I AM (Hebrew –YHVH), which I translated "The King of Everything." Why do you think God wants to reveal Himself to us through prayer as "The King of Everything?" Take some time to describe from the Bible what this "King of Everything" looks and acts like.

DAY 3: MOVING THE MIGHTY HAND OF GOD

3.1) In your climb up Prayer Mountain you will face huge mountains of opposition, just as Moses and the children of Israel did from a powerful Pharaoh who was not about to free them from slavery. What mountains of opposition stand in the way and keep you from the promises God has for you?

3.2) Take a few minutes and meditate on these promises from Exodus 6:6-8:

- *I will free you from the bondage of your enemies, sins, and addictions.*

- *I will redeem you through the blood of the Lamb, through my son Jesus who forgives all your sins.*

- *I will take you as my beloved children, and I will be your loving Father.*

- *I will bring you into my perfect promises for you just as I promised to your parents with uplifted hand and you will possess my Kingdom.*

What promises speak to you most during this season of your spiritual climb? Do these promises bring you hope as you look at the different mountains of opposition you are facing?

3.3) Prayer is the greatest means to access the promises of God for your life and empower you to overcome the lies of the "Pharaohs" you face. So take time right now to claim each of these promises over your life in prayer.

DAY 4: WHEN YOU'RE BETWEEN THE DEVIL AND THE DEEP BLUE SEA

4.1) Sometimes after great spiritual victories happen, you face your greatest spiritual battles. We see this in Day 4, where Moses and the children of Israel are trapped in a dead end. Describe an event in your life where you have seen this to be true.

4.2) In Exodus 14:13-14, we come to one of the greatest prayer points in Scripture: "Do not be afraid. Stand firm and you will see the deliverance the LORD will bring…you need only be still." Why do you think being "still" before the LORD is vital for your prayer life? List several reasons why it is so hard to "be still" in our culture.

4.3) The word "still" means to quiet yourself. From this meditation I share about how I use Revelation 5 to help me calm my fearful soul in order to be still. What are some elements from the description of Jesus found in this passage that would help you "be still" and watch your Great God bring you victory?

DAY 5: PLAY YOUR TAMBOURINE

5.1) Learning to "be still" in prayer allowed the Israelites to see the powerful salvation of God, bringing them through the parted waters of the Red Sea and safely to the other shore. From there they watched God's hand release the walls of water, destroying the pursuing Pharaoh and His army. This led to the first described corporate worship service recorded in Scripture (Ex. 15). Describe an event in your life where you praised God for His miraculous intervention.

5.2) Read the Song of Moses found in Exodus 15 and list several reasons why Moses and the children of Israel dance and sing praise before the LORD.

5.3) Do you agree with this statement in Day 5? "Moses teaches us that Prayer Mountain is a place saturated with praise and worship. One of the greatest ways to open up the Heavens and experience the presence of God is to sing, dance, shout, play whatever instrument you are able, and simply praise God for His daily gift of salvation given to you through His Son." If you agree, what are some practical ways you can turn your prayer times into a worship encounters that opens the gates of heaven?

WEEK 2: DAYS 6-10

DAY 6: TURNING THE BITTER INTO A BLESSING

6.1) Take a few moments and read Exodus 15 and notice the sharp contrast between praise and grumbling in this passage. Explain a time in your life where you went from gratitude to grumbling. What would you say is the source behind a grumbling or bitter spirit?

6.2) When we grumble and complain we are basically saying, "God we don't trust your leadership over us." Why is crying out to God in prayer as Moses did the solution to defeating a grumbling spirit?

6.3) After God shows Moses the solution to turn polluted water into pure, drinkable water, He declares these words: **"I am the LORD, who heals you,"** (Ex. 15:26). Describe a time in your life where "crying out" to God in prayer during a bitter time brought "healing" from the LORD.

DAY 7: OPENING HEAVEN FOR OTHERS

7.1) Moses is one of the greatest intercessors in the Bible. What do you think are some of the reasons he spent so much time praying for other people?

7.2) Many of the people Moses prayed for were people that opposed him. Why is it important to pray for and over our enemies? Give other biblical examples that would support this.

7.3) What is your reaction to this statement? **"Your prayers can change the destiny of countless people in our world."** Give some examples of where you have seen God use your prayers to transform lives.

7.4) Ask the Holy Spirit to place on your heart those He is calling you to open heaven for. Write their names in a journal or some place you can remember them in prayer. Daily bring them before the LORD and wait in anticipation for how He will work in their lives.

DAY 8: THE CRY OF YOUR HEART

8.1) *Think about this question asked in Day 8, "What is the deepest longing in your heart?" What would you say are the five deepest longings in our culture today? Are achieving any of these longings bringing a spirit of peace and contentment? As you read Exodus 33:12-23, why do you think Moses' greatest longing is for more of the presence of the LORD in his life? What experiences in his life brought him to cry out, "Show me Your glory!"*

8.2) *Consider this statement: "Once you taste the Presence of the Lord, you can't live without it." Have you found this true in your own journey of faith? Can you share other examples from Scripture or from people you know who have been "ruined," (in a good way) by the Presence of the LORD?*

8.3) *Do you think God will answer the prayer for more of His presence in our lives? Do you believe He will "show us Your glory," as He did for Moses? Is this is a prayer God loves to answer? Why or why not?*

DAY 9: WHAT THE LORD LOVES TO SAY

9.1) *Read the following verse slowly and carefully. Circle the words that speak to your heart:* **"The LORD, the LORD the compassionate and gracious God, slow to anger, abounding in love and faithfulness, maintaining love to thousands, and forgiving wickedness, rebellion and sin. Yet He does not leave the guilty unpunished; He punishes the children and their children for the sin of the fathers to the third and forth generation"** *(Exodus 34:6-7). Explain how the words you circled are speaking to you at this time?*

9.2) *As you again consider the words from Exodus 34:6-7, describe how Jesus is the fulfillment of these words. Give some examples from the life of Jesus that bring the words above to life.*

9.3) *What are some ways that help you listen to the voice of love from your Good Father? Share a time where you experienced the Father speaking words of love to you. Write a letter to yourself from a loving Father God; ask the Holy Spirit to take over your pen and unleash the Father's heart for you His child.*

DAY 10: FINAL WORDS FROM THE MOUNTAIN

10.1) *Take a few moments and read Psalm 90, which is titled, "A Prayer of Moses, the Man of God." What truths can you glean from these words of Moses that will help your prayer life?*

10.2) *In Day 10, I challenge you to memorize vs. 14:* **"Satisfy us in the morning with your unfailing love that we may sing for joy and be glad all our days."** *From Moses' perspective, the morning is a time for us to be filled up with the love of God, which results in days filled with joy. Have you found this to be true in your life? Can you give examples of a time in your life where His "unfailing love" experienced in morning prayer has carried you through the day? Or describe a day where there was no time to pray and what did that feel like?*

Elijah is an ordinary man who experiences drastic spiritual ups-and-downs. Yet, he learns to depend on God through prayer and, as a result, is used by God to turn a wayward nation back to Him.

CLIMBING WITH
ELIJAH

You don't need to be superhuman to pray.

Day 11

JUST LIKE US

> *Elijah was a man just like us.*
> – JAMES 5:17

Moses set a blistering pace for us during the first ten days of our climb up *Prayer Mountain*. His example, his *climbing*, sets such a lofty standard that is seems impossible for us to follow him. The next biblical figure whose amazing trail we will follow is Elijah. You might be thinking, "Isn't Elijah one of the greatest prophets ever, and we're supposed to be like him? Are you serious?"

James responds to this thought by saying: "*Elijah was a man just like us. He prayed earnestly that it would not rain, and it did not rain on the land for three and a half years. Again he prayed, and the heavens gave rain, and the earth produced its crops*" (5:17-18). True, Elijah is one of the pinnacle *Prayer Mountain* climbers; at times he even appears to be super human. Yet, James wants us to know he was human just like us, and if he can do it, we can do it as well.

Let's start by glancing at Elijah's background, his credentials so to speak.

"*Now Elijah the Tishbite, from Tishbe in Gilead*" (1 Kings 17:1).

That's it! That is all we know about Elijah's past. He is a mountain man from the small wilderness town of Tishbe, east of the Jordan River. We don't even know what tribe he's from or anything about his parents, other than they named him Elijah which means, "God is Yah" or "God is the great I AM." His parents must have believed in the true God of Israel, the God of Moses, Abraham, Isaac, and Jacob in one of the most evil times in Israel's history when the god Baal was worshiped.

Elijah's rough camel skin clothes reveal that he didn't grow up with position or privilege. He didn't have seminary training, nor did he pastor a mega church. My guess is he roamed around the rugged mountains as an introvert, learning in loneliness to cry out to God in prayer. He, like Moses, heard the voice of God in the solitude of the wilderness. He was a nobody from nowhere who learned to know God in an intimate way.

Over the years, I have found the greatest prayer warriors have come out of a place of deep loneliness and dark pain. These individuals are often ones who had no one else to cry out to but God. He is always faithful to hear the call of His needy children; He lifts them up on eagle's wings and uses them for His absolute glory. This was Elijah, and it can be you as well.

PONDER | MEDITATE | PRAY

PONDER 1 CORINTHIANS 1:27-29

But God chose the foolish things of the world to shame the wise; God chose the weak things of the world to shame the strong. He chose the lowly things of this world and the despised things–and the things that are not–to nullify the things that are so, that no one may boast before Him.

MEDITATE ON AND PRAY INTO 1 CORINTHIANS 1:27-29

Praise God:

– for being a God who lifts-up the weak

– for His power and strength

Tell God:

– about your sins and worries, give them to Him

Thank God:

- for using the weak, for listening to your prayers

Ask God:

– to provide you with discipline to continue climbing

– to show you ways to glorify Him and enjoy Him

EXTENDED STUDY QUESTIONS: PAGE 108

*It is in private prayer
that we come to know
the living LORD.*

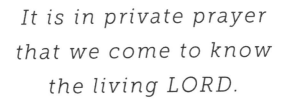

Day 12

PRAYERS IN PRIVATE

> *Now Elijah the Tishbite, from Tishbe in Gilead, said to Ahab,*
> *'As the LORD, the God of Israel lives, whom I serve, there will be*
> *neither dew nor rain in the next few years except at my word.'*
>
> – 1 KINGS 17:1

It has often been said, "What you are in private will reveal who you are in public." From I Kings 17:1, three details are revealed about the private life of Elijah:

- He knew the living LORD through private prayer.
- His boldness came out of his relationship with the LORD.
- He prayed the Word.

It is in private prayer that we come to know a living LORD. The years Elijah spent in the rocky mountains of Gilead brought him before a personal LORD. His spirit was made alive and was in tune to the Father's voice. In a world of constant noise clamoring for our attention, it is vital that we spend time seeking the Face of our Father in private. This time will be the most important part of your day and will bring you life like nothing else can. Once you have tasted a relationship with the Father in private prayer, this time will become your consuming passion.

For various reasons, I grew up as a people pleaser. This form of idolatry, rooted in pride, will suck the life out of you and make you weak. For me, the only way to overcome this stumbling block is a daily encounter with the Holy King of the Universe. From my reading about Elijah's life, I speculate he was shy and likely enjoyed solitude. So for him to confront the ruthless, wicked king of Israel had to be a supernatural empowering of God. Ahab could have easily had his henchmen hang him right there when he prophesied the bad news of no rain. Yet, as a result of his relationship with the Almighty, he became a bold God pleaser, not a man pleaser.

The third thing that pops out of this text is that Elijah knew and prayed the Word of God. How could he be so bold in his proclamation about no rain? He knew Moses' words from Deuteronomy 11:16:

"Be careful, or you will be enticed to turn away and worship other gods and bow down to them. Then the LORD's anger will burn against you, and He will shut the heavens so that it will not rain and the ground will yield no produce, and you will soon perish from the good land the LORD is giving you' (Deut. 11:16).

Elijah kept the Word of God in his heart and interpreted his times correctly, as the Northern tribes of Israel had turned away from the living God to Baal worship. In praying the Word, the Holy Spirit moved Elijah to act and confront the wickedness in public. His love for the LORD, His Word, and His people moved Elijah to confront Ahab with the truth. His private prayers would lead to a powerful public display of the glorious fame of the Living LORD and awaken a slumbering Israel to the only true God. (*Read I Kings 17-19 for the full account of this amazing story.*)

Make a commitment to seek the living Lord in private until you find His transforming presence.

PONDER | MEDITATE | PRAY

PONDER ISAIAH 55:6-7

Seek the LORD while He may be found; call on Him while He is near. Let the wicked forsake his way and the evil man his thoughts. Let him turn to the LORD, and He will have mercy on him and to our God for He will freely pardon.

MEDITATE ON AND PRAY INTO ISAIAH 55:6-7

Praise God:

– for allowing us to approach Him in prayer

Tell God:

– about the "noises" that distract you from Him

Thank God:

- for providing His Word and revealing Himself through it

– for His mercy

Ask God:

– to help you understand, interpret, and discern His word

– for His help with your particular needs

EXTENDED STUDY QUESTIONS: PAGES 108-109

You can depend on God.

Day 13

I AM YOUR PROVISION

Then the word of the LORD came to Elijah: 'Leave here, turn eastward and hide in the Kerith Ravine, east of the Jordan. You will drink from the brook, and I have ordered the ravens to feed you there.'

– 1 KINGS 17:2-4

As I write day thirteen, I'm overwhelmed at the faithful provision of our Father God. Some time ago, our Good Father asked my wife Patty and I to leave my position as senior pastor, and my secure salary, to follow Him into the unknown and launch *Oceans Ministries*. The vision He had inscribed on our hearts for years was to make the love of the Father known to spiritual and physical orphans around the world.

One of the stipulations God placed on our hearts was that we refrain from seeking financial support, but rather totally trust Him to provide for all our needs. We were in the middle of the most costly seasons of our lives, with two kids in college and one in high school, yet we heard His voice loud and clear.

Right away during this crazy call on our lives, God brought me back to this story of Elijah and the brook of Kerith. The Holy Spirit deeply ministered to me as I contemplated how God raised Elijah up to confront wicked Ahab and then sent him back across the Jordan into the wilderness to live again in solitude, where he was to trust alone in the LORD to be his provision. Before Elijah would experience the glorious revival on Mount Carmel, he first needed to learn to trust at Kerith.

Notice in the story, Elijah wasn't led to a flowing river but rather a trickling brook that provided just enough water to sustain him. God also chose to provide a bird, which was unclean according to Israel's purity laws, to bring Elijah food. What a journey of trust Elijah was sent on, but one that was essential for growth in his prayer life and dependence on God for what was ahead.

I'm convinced our Good Father desires for us to come to a place of absolute dependence on Him, where we cry out to Him alone to meet our daily needs. This story of Elijah gave me hope for the journey God had called my family to walk. As I write these words, I realize that the months have turned to years since we were called to "step out of the boat" and trust in Him. Has it always been easy? Absolutely not. Like Peter, I took my eyes off of Jesus as I contemplated the future and financial security. I started to sink, but Jesus was always there to grab me and redirect my eyes to His glorious, loving face. Now I can testify with great praise that Abba Father is enough, and He has provided for all our needs abundantly. In fact, this very morning we received a sizable donation from someone who has never given before but was prompted by the Spirit to give to Oceans. My eyes were filled with tears of praise and thanksgiving as I shared the news of this gift with my wife.

For three years, Elijah experienced the miraculous provision of His loving Father. His journey should motivate us all to cry out in faith to a Father who knows exactly what we need and rejoices in providing for His children. I'm not sure what your need is at this time, but tell your Father about it and trust in His great goodness to meet you at your Kerith.

PONDER | MEDITATE | PRAY

PONDER PHILIPPIANS 4:19

And my God will meet all your needs according to His glorious riches in Christ Jesus.

MEDITATE ON AND PRAY INTO PHILIPPIANS 4:19

Praise God:

– for His glorious provision

Tell God:

– about the things you depend on instead of Him, give them to Him

Thank God:

- for the way(s) He has provided for you

Ask God:

– to help you keep your eyes on Him

– to help you discern His leading

– for continued provision

❖ EXTENDED STUDY QUESTIONS: PAGE 109

God loves answering prayers that stretch into the supernatural; this is how He grows His Kingdom.

Day 14

STRETCHING INTO THE SUPERNATURAL

> *The LORD heard Elijah's cry, and the boy's life returned to him, and he lived.*
>
> – 1 KINGS 17:22

Your journey up *Prayer Mountain* will lead you to some chasms that are seemingly impossible to cross over. However, you will learn as you climb in prayer that God loves to show up when the mountain seems impassable. An important part of your education in prayer during your climb will be to develop a deeper trust in the supernatural provision and power of our God.

By the brook of Kerith, Elijah learned the supernatural provision of God in the midst of a drought. When the brook dried up, he trusted the LORD's leading when he was told to go on a seventy-five-mile journey through the desert into enemy territory, to a place called Zarephath. In this place of Baal worship, God had a divine appointment for Elijah. There, a widow and her son were cooking their last meal; and this was the place where God would take care of His prophet (I Kings 17:7-24).

Upon meeting the widow, Elijah approached her and asked for food. It is not surprising that she protested and proceeded to explain that she was making one last meal for herself and her son. Yet, Elijah responded: *"First make a small loaf of bread for me from what you have and bring it to me, and then make something for yourself and your son. For this is what the Lord, the God of Israel, says: 'The jar of flour will not be used up and the jug of oil will not run dry until the day the Lord sends rain on the land.'"* (vs. 13-14). Wow, talk about bold words!

God was true to His word, as just enough oil and flour remained in the jars until the rain came. Sadly, in the midst of this heavenly provision, darkness invaded this simple home, and the widow's son becomes sick and dies. The widow, obviously in unbearable pain, lashes out at Elijah. Elijah reacts by taking the boy in his arms, lays him on his bed, shuts the door, and cries out to God. Now, to this point in biblical history, there is no record of anyone being resurrected from the dead. Yet, Elijah steps out in faith, wrestles with God, and asks God to do the unthinkable. We read that the prayer is not answered right away, but Elijah doesn't give up as the text says: "*Then he stretched himself out on the boy three times and cried to the LORD, 'LORD my God, let this boy's life return to him!'*" (vs. 21).

All of Elijah's experiences in the school of prayer had grown his faith. His passionate plea was heard. The Father was pleased by his stretching faith and breathed life again into the boy. Can you imagine the celebration in that house when the boy hugged his mom? Also, notice how God is glorified in this moment as the woman responds by saying: "*Now I know that you are a man of God and that the word of the LORD from your mouth is the truth*" (vs. 24).

God loves answering prayers that stretch into the supernatural; this is how He grows His Kingdom. We will discuss this more as we watch Jesus and the disciples climb *Prayer Mountain* and bring down heaven. But the challenge before us, in a culture that denies the supernatural power of God, is to stretch out in prayer and believe there is nothing our God cannot do, even raise the dead!

PONDER | MEDITATE | PRAY

PONDER LUKE 1:37

For nothing is impossible for God.

MEDITATE ON AND PRAY INTO LUKE 1:37

Praise God:

– that He answers prayers with His supernatural power

Tell God:

– about your sins and worries, give them to Him

Thank God:

- that nothing is impossible for Him

Ask God:

– for faith to ask for the impossible

– to help you with your impossible problem

❖ EXTENDED STUDY QUESTIONS: PAGES 109-110

❖

Through prayer,
God revealed Himself
to unbelievers.

❖

Day 15

THE PRAYER CHALLENGE

The god who answers by fire – He is God.

– 1 KINGS 18:24

If you're ever in Israel, try to spend some time on Mount Carmel. Not only does it have a fantastic view of the Jezreel Valley, where many historic battles were fought, but it is the location of one of the most dramatic scenes in biblical history. It is on Mount Carmel that Elijah beckoned a prayer challenge with King Ahab and the 450 prophets of Baal. Every time I'm there, I read I Kings 18:16-46, and imagine myself in the midst of that great scene.

A solo Elijah summoned the Baal worshipers, led by wicked King Ahab and his demonic wife Jezebel, and challenged them to a prayer contest. The rules were: build an altar, put a bull on it, and call out to your god. The god/God who answered by fire is the true One to be worshiped and followed. The bewitched followers of Baal agreed to the challenge, and all day they prayed, danced around the altar, even mutilated their flesh to invoke Baal, the god of fire and storm, to show up. Elijah made sport of it and did some trash talking, telling them to shout louder because their god might be sleeping or going to the bathroom. After several exhausting hours, there was no answer from the fire god.

Elijah then got busy repairing an old altar to the LORD that was in ruins. He placed the bull on it and, just to up the ante, doused the sacrifice with gallons of water to prove no trickery. Notice his simple short prayer:

"O LORD, God of Abraham, Isaac and Israel, let it be known today that you are God in Israel and that I am your servant and have done all these things at your command. Answer me, O LORD, answer me,

so these people will know that you, O LORD, are God, and that you are turning their hearts back again" (vs. 36-37).

As you reflect on this prayer, which takes about fifteen seconds to pray, you notice it is focused on one thing, *"So these people will know that you, O LORD, are God..."* The people were giving their lives over to a made-up deity who was destroying the Northern Tribes of Israel. Elijah's passion, which is God's passion, is that they would come back to Him, the only true God. When you pray God's heart, you are assured an answer will follow as was experienced on Mount Carmel!

"Then the fire of the LORD fell and burned up the sacrifice, the wood, the stones and the soil, and also licked up the water in the trench" (vs. 38).

God undeniably showed-up the "fire god," Baal, at his own game, and the people face-planted before the glory of God and cried out over and over again: *"The LORD He is God!"* (vs. 39).

Every time I read this story on Mount Carmel, I'm convicted of my need to pray for the glory of Jesus Christ to fall like fire and awaken my own heart. I'm also convicted to pray for the blinded culture I live in, which is filled with worship of countless false gods. Yet, in the midst of this incredible story, it is the simple and effective prayer prayed for the glory of God's name, and His name alone, that I remember most.

Elijah, *a man just like us,* beckons us to combat our idol-filled hearts with a simple prayer pronouncing the LORD's glory and begging Him once again to reveal Himself to a lost generation. If God can answer Elijah's prayer so powerfully, why not ours?

PONDER | MEDITATE | PRAY

PONDER JAMES 5:16

Therefore confess your sins to each other and pray for each other so that you may be healed. The prayer of a righteous man is powerful and effective.

MEDITATE ON AND PRAY INTO JAMES 5:16

Praise God:

– for His power and might, for His mercy

Tell God:

– about your idols, give them to Him

Thank God:

- for the ways He has showed-up in your life

Ask God:

– to remove any idol(s) from your heart

– to heal your spirit

– to reveal Himself to a lost generation

❧ EXTENDED STUDY QUESTIONS: PAGE 110

❖

*Don't give up praying
even when you don't see
results immediately.*

❖

16

Day 16

PRAYING THE PROMISES

Elijah was a man just like us. He prayed earnestly that it would not rain,
and it did not rain on the land for three and a half years. Again he prayed,
and the heavens gave rain, and the earth produced its crops.

– JAMES 5:17-18

I am blessed to claim a corner of my basement as a prayer room where I can connect to my loving Abba Father. When you walk-in you will notice a blue-padded, glider-rocker which belonged to my Grandma Spykstra. For me, it is a sacred place to sit and pray because it is the same seat where my grandma spent hours praying for her family. I was overjoyed when the chair was gifted to me, as it is a reminder of the power of persistent prayer.

When my grandma passed away, my father shared with me a stack of prayer journals that belonged to her. As I read them, I was overwhelmed by the years of intercessory prayers recorded for her children and grandchildren. She prayed fervently for humanly-speaking impossible situations that plagued some family members. She daily prayed that each of her grandkids would follow after Jesus as their LORD and Savior. She never gave up, and even though she didn't get to see all the answers to her prayers before she went to Jesus, Jesus was faithful and answered the cries of her heart, as I can affirm after reading her daily entries.

In a way, my grandma had that same spirit Elijah did as he kept asking and praying for the impossible. Elijah, after winning the prayer challenge against the prophets of Baal, went to work praying for much-needed rain. In fact, he was so sure that the clear skies were about to become cloudy and bring torrential rains that he told wicked King Ahab to get ready because he could already hear the *"sound of heavy rain"* (1 Kings 18:41). Elijah was certain the rain was on its way, even though not a drop had fallen for three and a half years. Continuing to climb higher on Mount Carmel, and on his personal *prayer mountain*, Elijah reached the summit of the mount and *"bent down to the ground and put his face between his knees,"* (18:42).

Elijah demonstrated how we access the promises of God's Word. He believed rain was on the way, and, by faith, he knew prayer was the means to bring down the promises. In a fetal position like a needy child, he pleads with Father God for rain. After a prayer session, Elijah tells someone to go look towards the Mediterranean Sea for a rain cloud; there was nothing. This scene played out over and over again with the same report, "Nothing!" Still, the elder prophet kept at it, his bearded face between his knees, calling out for his Father to send rain.

Finally, after the seventh time, it was reported, *"A cloud as small as a man's hand is rising from the sea,"* (vs. 44). The sighting was enough for Elijah. In his mind, the prayer was answered. He was so confident, he got off the ground and told Ahab to hitch-up his horses and head down from the mountain so he wouldn't get stuck in the mud. Sure enough, the clouds darkened, and the heavens opened in response to a righteous man's prayers.

I love how the chapter ends with Elijah outrunning the chariot of Ahab *"in the power of the LORD,"* (vs. 46). Elijah experienced God's glory, first by fire and next by rain. His spirit was overwhelmed and overflowing, and I can just imagine him raising his arms in victory as he blazed by Ahab's chariot.

In the morning as I sit in my grandma's prayer rocker, I'm reminded to keep praying for the rain, even in the midst of a spiritual drought. A day will come when the glorious cloud of God's presence will respond to your prayers and mine. I would encourage you today and every day to find a place to pray and put your prayers in the hands of a promise-keeping Father God. Please don't stop until you see the cloud on the horizon.

PONDER | MEDITATE | PRAY

PONDER LUKE 18:7-8

And will not God bring justice for His chosen ones, who cry out to Him day and night? Will He keep putting them off? I tell you, He will see that they get justice, and quickly.

MEDITATE ON AND PRAY INTO LUKE 18:7-8

Praise God:

– for showing up in fire and rain at Mount Carmel

– for the storm

Tell God:

– about your needs, give them to Him

– that you trust in His timing

Thank God:

- for His justice and provision

Ask God:

– for discipline to spend time in prayer every day

– to answers to your needs

– for patience and perseverance

– for His peace

❖ EXTENDED STUDY QUESTIONS: PAGE 111

Even when you can't pray, your Father will not give up on you.

Day 17

WHEN YOU CAN'T PRAY

I have had enough LORD…take my life…
I'm no better than my ancestors.
– 1 KINGS 19:4

Have you ever had days, weeks, or even months when you were so tired, beat-up, and weary of life's battles that prayer becomes almost impossible? Take comfort, so did the great prophet Elijah.

Elijah had just witnessed the power of God move to answer his prayers on Mount Carmel, as fire and rain came in response to his calling out to God. Thousands had been moved by what happened there, and many came back to the LORD as the only true God. You'd think he'd be taking victory laps around Ahab's palace, shouting praises to God. But this was not the case, as we read in 1 Kings 19:1-3. Instead, fear overtook Elijah when he got wind of the report that Ahab's wife, Jezebel, was incensed by what happened up on the mountain and had called for his head.

The enemy knows right when to move in and attack after a great work of God. In our minds, we think that after such a great move of the Spirit, hearts will soften and turn to the Lord. A revival will flood the church, and powerful transformation will take place! But then random things begin to happen; unexpected events occur in the form of emails, phone calls, job losses, sickness, or depression. Discouragements like these can overwhelm the soul.

Elijah might have thought that once Queen Jezebel heard all that happened on Mount Carmel, she would be humbled and beckon Elijah to the palace for a personal time of prayer and repentance. Instead, this fiery queen was enraged by the fires of hell and planned to obliterate the movement. Elijah was overcome with fear and this time, instead of standing his ground in prayer, he fled to the desert.

In the wilderness, he found a tree and offered what he thought was his last prayer: *"I have had enough, LORD…take my life…I'm not better than my ancestors"* (1 Kings 19:4). He was burned out. He was beat up. He was filled with guilt for running away from the battle. He wanted out, so he took a long nap hoping not to wake up.

What happens next reveals the unfailing love of God for His children that fail Him. The Father sent an angel to cook some heaven-baked bread to renew Elijah's struggling body and spirit. The bread was so satisfying that after Elijah indulged, he fell back asleep. Once again the angel came, brought more bread, and encouraged Elijah to eat because his work was not done. He had a journey before him to the Mountain of God, and he needed the heavenly food for strength (vs. 5-8).

I too have experienced seasons of discouragement and fear when all I could pray was, "I want out, I can't do this any more." But I've found that when I don't have any more energy to pray, the Father sends His Holy Spirit to feed my weary soul. It is so reassuring to know when you hit those seasons in life, your Father never gives up on you. He sends messengers from heaven to restore your soul and refuel you with life that comes from His Spirit. When all you are able to do is groan in pain, your Father gives you great prayer warriors, the Holy Spirit and His Son Jesus, to pray on your behalf. It is good to remember when you can't pray, He takes over and carries your life in His good hands.

PONDER | MEDITATE | PRAY

PONDER ROMANS 8:26, 34

The Spirit helps us in our weakness. We do not know what we ought to pray for, but the Spirit Himself intercedes for us with groans that words cannot express…Christ Jesus, who died–more than that, who was raised to life–is at the right hand of God and is interceding for us.

MEDITATE ON AND PRAY INTO ROMANS 8:26, 34

Praise God:

– for helping us in our weakness and difficulties

Tell God:

– about your difficulties, give them to Him

Thank God:

- for not giving up on you, for interceding on your behalf

– for carrying you through difficult seasons in life

Ask God:

– for strength to continue during good times and bad

– to show you what to pray for

EXTENDED STUDY QUESTIONS: PAGES 111-112

It is in prayerful solitude that we can hear God's gentle whisper.

Day 18

FINDING GOD IN A CAVE

And after the fire came a gentle whisper.
When Elijah heard it, he pulled his cloak over his face
and went out and stood at the mouth of the cave.
— I KINGS 19:12-13

While pastoring in Southern California, I stumbled across a retreat center called Prayer Mountain. It was a fascinating place developed by a pastor from South Korea who turned a mountain into a sanctuary for prayer. In the mountain, he dug out several caves that would hold anywhere from one to thirty people. It was one of my favorite places to pray; it was quiet, the temperature remained the same, and I felt free from all the distractions of the sometimes-crazy world of ministry. After spending a day in the solitude of the cave, I felt renewed and refreshed by the presence of the Lord. I was ready to go back down and live into my calling.

I have no doubt that Elijah was ready for a cave experience far away from the spiritual battle he faced in Israel. After being refreshed by the bread and water from heaven, God sent Elijah on a forty-day hike through the desert to the famous Mount Horeb. This was the place where God spiritually betrothed Israel and Moses delivered the Ten Commandments. Moses also climbed this mountain in order to plead with God to forgive Israel's sins after they broke their vow by worshiping a golden calf. In this place of powerful symbolism and historic significance, Elijah finds a cave in which to rest after his long journey. It was in this cave, more than likely the same one in which Moses experienced the glory of God, that God chose to speak to His servant.

This truly is an astonishing story. The voice of the LORD awakens Elijah from his sleep and tells him to go out to the mouth of the cave so that he may witness the Glory of God's presence as He passes by.

I can imagine Elijah waiting outside the cave and wondering what the presence of God would look like. First, a powerful wind tore apart the mountain. Next, a mighty earthquake shook it violently. Finally, a fire appeared. But the text says the LORD was not in the wind, earthquake, or fire (1 Kings 19:8-13). Rather the LORD chose to speak in a "gentle whisper" to His weary servant (vs. 13).

Why a *gentle whisper*? Because our Good Father knows just how to speak to us in our time of need. Elijah was still struggling with God over what appeared to be a failed ministry experience. He feels all is lost as he is the only one left in Israel that fears the LORD, and now his life is hanging in the balance as well (vs. 14). I believe it was a gentle whisper of love that entered his ears and began to sooth his troubled soul.

Our Father's heart is filled with overwhelming love and compassion, and He longs for us to hear this. Many times, it is in prayer that we are in tune to His gentle whisper; a whisper of love that brings deep healing to our hurting soul.

In the midst of your spiritual battles and discouragement, your Father longs to gently whisper His love to you. He is waiting for you to come to His Holy Mountain and find a quiet place where you can hear the whisper of His voice.

PONDER | MEDITATE | PRAY

PONDER ISAIAH 30:18

Yet the LORD longs to be gracious to you; He rises to show you compassion. For the LORD is a God of justice. Blessed are all who wait for Him!

MEDITATE ON AND PRAY INTO ISAIAH 30:18

Praise God:

– for being gracious and just

Tell God:

– that you want to hear His voice

Thank God:

- for His love

– for carrying you through difficult seasons in life

Ask God:

– for strength

– to speak to you

– to be able to hear His whisper

❖ EXTENDED STUDY QUESTIONS: PAGE 112

Ask your Father to bring people into your life to pray with.

Day 19

FINDING A PRAYER PARTNER

> *...and anoint Elisha, son of Shaphat from Abel
> Meholah to succeed you as prophet.*
> – 1 KINGS 19:16

During the three and a half years in which Elijah was called as a prophet of the Lord to confront Ahab and expose the false god of Baal, Elijah was pretty much a loner. But on Mount Horeb, God's *gentle whisper* instructed Elijah to invest himself in Elisha, who would become another powerful prophet used by God.

Elijah was called to anoint Elisha with the same mantle of the Holy Spirit that was on Elijah. Part of this anointing would be to teach the young prophet about daily living in the presence of God's Spirit through prayer. Though there are no specific texts that show the two men praying together, there is no doubt in my mind that Elisha was schooled in the art of prayer as this is essential for any prophet who hears from the LORD and speaks on His behalf.

I believe Elijah and Elisha formed an intimate spiritual bond in prayer, so much so that when God called Elijah home in a chariot of fire, Elisha did not leave Elijah's side–even when Elijah pleaded for his brother to let him journey on alone. When Elijah saw Elisha would not be deterred, he allowed him to follow and asked, *"What can I do for you before I am taken from you?"* (2 Kings 2:9). Elisha's prayer request was that God would give him a *double portion* of the Holy Spirit that was upon Elijah.

Wow! Elisha was thirsty for as much of God's presence as he could get and learned from Elijah to be bold in prayer. God honored this audacious request. After watching Elijah be swept away by the chariot of fire, Elisha picked up Elijah's prayer mantle and was filled to overflowing with the Spirit of God.

The stories of Elisha's life in 2 Kings record how he continued the work Elijah started. They are some of my favorites! God allowed Elisha to double the miracles performed by his mentor. This is fruitful discipleship birthed through prayer.

I too have found that effective discipleship transpires on your knees with others. Praying with another person or a group of people invites the presence of God into relationships, which will have a transforming impact on those praying together.

As a young pastor, God brought a man named Brian into my life, and he asked if I'd meet with him once a week for prayer. I agreed to the idea and after a breakfast at I-Hop, time was spent praying together. Sometimes it was a bit awkward praying at the restaurant, so eventually we moved to his truck in the parking lot for the prayer part. The Holy Spirit blessed those times, and soon other men asked to join us. Since we couldn't all fit in his pickup, we relocated to my home where we would weekly cry out to the Lord. Father God moved in each of our hearts, and powerful ministry flowed out of those early morning prayers. Wherever God has moved me in ministry, I know the first step I need to take is to find another brother to pray with.

In your climb up *Prayer Mountain*, I encourage you to ask your Father to bring people into your life to pray with. Start with your family members and watch what He does. Next, ask Him to reveal one other person He wants you to join in prayer with. Get ready for the *double portions* to follow.

PONDER | MEDITATE | PRAY

PONDER MATTHEW 18:19-20

*Again, I tell you that if two of you on earth agree about
anything you ask for, it will be done for you by my Father in
heaven. For where two or three come together in my name,
there am I with them.*

MEDITATE ON AND PRAY INTO MATTHEW 18:19-20

Praise God:

– for His plans for your life

Tell God:

– about the things that keep you from spending time with Him

– that you desire to have a prayer partner

Thank God:

– for His promise of answered prayers

Ask God:

– to bring someone into your life that you can pray with

– for a double portion of His Spirit

❖ EXTENDED STUDY QUESTIONS: PAGES 112-113

*Prepare your heart
for an intimate
encounter with Jesus.*

Day 20

PRAYING INTO
THE PROPHECY

> *See, I will send you the prophet Elijah before*
> *that great and dreadful day of the LORD comes.*
> *He will turn the hearts of the fathers to their children,*
> *and the hearts of the children to their fathers....*
> – MALACHI 4:5-6

The Old Testament ends with this powerful prophecy reminding us of the anointed prophet Elijah, and how the Spirit, which dwelt in him, is able to bring healing to families and the broken hearted. The *great and dreadful day of the LORD* is the coming judgment, and yet God has ordained another opportunity for repentance. Just as the prophet Elijah called Israel to return to the one true God, God will raise up others to be the voice of Elijah in our day.

The New Testament begins with the powerful preaching of John the Baptist, who called the people to repent and turn back to God. John baptized all those who heeded this invitation and put a spotlight on Jesus, *"The Lamb of God who takes away the sin of the world,"* (John 1:29). Jesus by His life, death, and resurrection opened the door for us to return to the Father's presence. Accepting this gift through faith in Jesus brings healing into all of our relationships. He is the one who *"will turn the hearts of the fathers to their children, and the hearts of the children to their fathers,"* (Malachi 4:6).

I believe the spirit of Elijah didn't stop with John the Baptist, but it continues to come to *"restore all things,"* (Matt. 17:11). The Father desires to make Himself known to us through Jesus, whose sole mission in life was to make the Father known (John 17:1-3). Accept this gift and claim this truth: you are children of God and have access to

God. Go ahead and let your *"Abba Father"* (Romans 8:15) know what is on your heart in prayer.

Praying into this prophecy over the years led me to found *Oceans Ministries*, with the sole purpose of **making the Father known**. So many of us live like we are physical or spiritual orphans, and yet the Father desires that we be filled with the Spirit and live like we are sons and daughters of King Jesus. The heart of *Oceans Ministries* is to restore hearts across the street and across the world to the Heavenly Father. Countless individuals of all ages, races, and genders have experienced father wounds from their earthly dad, which has inhibited their ability to receive the love their Heavenly Father desires to freely give them. Through counseling and serving in the established church, working with prisoners in the states and orphans in Africa, as well interacting with the homeless and downcast in the inner city, I have realized that we are all broken and in need of restoration to our Good Father.

What a blessing to testify that I have seen and experienced the spirit of Elijah being poured out in the darkest of places, illuminating the Father's love through a new revelation of the glorious work of Jesus Christ and the Holy Spirit. I have found in my own life, through seasons of prayer, confession of sin, and forgiveness through the cross of Jesus, a healing that flooded my soul from an encounter with my Abba Father. I'm convinced that knowing God as our Father is the most important relationship in our life. When we live as His children, we live the way we were created to live–as sons and daughters of the King!

Pray with me into this prophecy of Malachi 4:5-6, that the spirit of Elijah would be revived in our day and restore our hearts to our true Father.

PONDER | MEDITATE | PRAY

PONDER ROMANS 8:15

For you did not receive a spirit of fear that makes you a slave again to fear, but you received the Spirit of sonship. And by Him we cry, 'Abba Father.'

MEDITATE ON AND PRAY INTO ROMANS 8:15

Praise God:

– for being your Abba Father

Tell God:

– about your brokenness, give it to Him

– that you want to know Him

Thank God:

– for showing Himself to you through Jesus

Ask God:

– to bring revival into your heart and the hearts of those around you

EXTENDED STUDY QUESTIONS: PAGE 113

CLIMBING WITH
ELIJAH

QUESTIONS FOR
EXTENDED STUDY

WEEK 3: DAYS 11-15

DAY 11: JUST LIKE US

11.1) Do you ever feel like you are not qualified to pray? You don't have the right training, biblical knowledge, or credentials to pray effectively. Why do you think James says, "Elijah was a man just like us," (5:17)? Do you see any significance in the fact that the Bible doesn't give us any background data about Elijah's past life?

11.2) All we know about Elijah's past is that he is a "Tishbite, from Tishbe in Gilead,"(1 Kings 17:1), which is a rugged mountainous area that was sparsely populated. Use your sanctified imagination and describe how Elijah's obscurity and his rural upbringing developed his prayer life?

11.3) Take a few minutes and think about your past and upbringing. How can the circumstances of your life be used by the Father to draw you to Him in prayer? Have you had times of loneliness or suffering where the only place to turn was to God in prayer? Describe one of these times and how it either led you closer to God or maybe away from Him? Would you agree with this statement in the devotional: **"Over the years I have found the greatest prayer warriors have come out of a place of deep loneliness and dark pain."** *Why or why not?*

DAY 12: PRAYERS IN PRIVATE

12.1) In 1 Kings 17:1, God speaks these words through Elijah to wicked King Abab: **"As the LORD, the God of Israel lives, whom I serve, there will be neither dew nor rain in the next few years except at my word."** *Describe how Elijah's private prayer time would have given him the courage to prophesy this. Do you agree with the statement: "What you are in private will reveal what you are in public," why or why not?*

12.2) List several reasons why your private prayer times will help you live out your faith boldly in the world. What are some obstacles that have hindered your private prayer times? How does life go when your private prayer times are missed?

12.3) Elijah is able to confront Ahab because of his private prayer life and his understanding of the Word of God. Why do you think your private prayers and knowing the Word of God are so important? Can you give any examples where through prayer and God's Word you were empowered to live out your faith boldly?

DAY 13: I AM YOUR PROVISION

13.1) After Elijah confronts wicked Ahab, God tells Elijah to go and hide in the wilderness and that the LORD will provide miraculously. How do you think God was using this to grow Elijah in his prayer life? What are some words that you would use to describe how God was growing Elijah through this radical event?

13.2) How do you think the daily provision of water from the brook and the raven's delivery of bread and meat in the morning and night strengthened Elijah's prayer life? (1 Kings 17:2-6). Can you give other examples from Scripture where God provided miraculously for His people? What does this say about the character of Father God?

13.3) Share a time in your life, or in the life of someone you know, where Father God provided in a miraculous way? How has God used this event to strengthen your trust in Him and grow you in your prayer life? Is there something right now that God is asking you to do that would require you to step out in faith and trust Him to be your provision? If so, spend time asking God to give you faith to trust Him with your life and strength to follow His lead.

DAY 14: STRETCHING INTO THE SUPERNATURAL

14.1) Please take some time and read 1 Kings 17:7-24. As you read and ponder this amazing story what comes to your mind about lessons Elijah had learned about prayer that prepared him for what he encountered at Zarephath?

14.2) Why do you think God led Elijah into enemy territory, the center of Baal worship, to live with the widow and her son? What did the provision of endless oil and flour demonstrate to the widow and her son about the heart of God?

14.3) We live in a world that tends to deny the supernatural, why do you think that is so? As you read about the death of the widow's son and Elijah's prayer for him in verses 19-21, how would you describe his prayer? From verse 24, what is the result of God answering Elijah's prayer? Do you believe that Father God wants to show His supernatural glory through your prayers as well, why or why not?

DAY 15: THE PRAYER CHALLENGE

15.1) Elijah had grown deeply in the school of prayer for three plus years and was ready to be an apparent underdog in the contest on Mount Carmel (1 Kings 18:16-39). Describe ways that prayer molds the heart to be courageous in the midst of impossible battles.

15.2) Read Elijah's simple/quick prayer in verses 36–37. How would you summarize the intent of his prayer? Why was he certain that his prayer would be answered? If we have the same motive in our prayers, can we live with the same certainty of our prayers being answered, why or why not?

15.3) When I read this passage about the Prayer Challenge between the prophets of Baal and Elijah, I'm confronted by my sin and the sin of the culture in which I live in. How I need the fire of the Holy Spirit to reveal the idols in my heart that keep me from knowing the true God. What are the idols in your heart that are keeping you from an encounter with the living God? James 5:16 states: **"Therefore confess your sins to each other and pray for each other so that you may be healed. The prayer of a righteous man is powerful and effective."** Find someone to practice this verse with and believe that forgiveness and healing will come from the Father, through His son Jesus, in the power of the Holy Spirit.

WEEK 4: DAYS 16-20

DAY 16: PRAYING THE PROMISES

16.1) As you read 1 Kings 18:41-46, you realize Elijah's prayer work is not done. After God's glorious answer to his prayers for fire to come on the altar, he now pleads for the three and a half year drought to end through the gift of rain. From the text, how many times did Elijah ask his helper to look and see if rain clouds were on the horizon? What do you think this says about the importance of persistent prayer?

16.2) Why is it that God doesn't always answer our prayers the first time we ask Him? Can you give examples from other stories in the Bible where prayers were not answered right away but God honored their perseverance, as they believed God to keep His promises?

16.3) I shared in Day 16 about how my Grandma Spykstra was a fervent prayer warrior for her family. As I read her prayer journals, I noticed that some of her requests were not answered until after she passed away and went to be with Jesus. What are your thoughts on the importance of praying even when you don't see immediate results? Can you give examples of answered promises after seasons of persistent prayer in your own life?

DAY 17: WHEN YOU CAN'T PRAY

17.1) What were the factors in 1 Kings 19:1-6 that brought Elijah to the breaking point where he asked God to take his life? Have you ever experienced seasons of deep discouragement when it was to hard to pray and you felt abandoned by God? Describe how those seasons felt and your struggle with your prayer life?

17.2) As you read this account of Elijah's dark night of the soul, where does God show up in the story? Why isn't it enough to give Elijah hope to go on? How does God respond to Elijah's going back to sleep? What does that say to you about God's love for you even in your darkest times when you can't pray?

17.3) At the end of Day 17 you were directed to ponder and pray Romans 8:26,34. As you meditated on those two verses, how does the fact that the Holy Spirit and Jesus Himself are praying for you when you can't pray give you hope and assurance in your darkest seasons?

DAY 18: FINDING GOD IN A CAVE

18.1) We read in 1 Kings 19:7-18 that God leads Elijah on a forty day journey to Mountain Horeb to meet him in a cave. Why would God choose to bring Elijah to this specific place to meet with Him? Are there sacred places where God has brought you where you can connect with Him better? If so, explain why?

18.2) Why do you think it was the "gentle whisper" rather than the "violent wind, earthquake, or fire," that grabbed Elijah's attention and moved him to the front of the cave? (vs. 11-12). How has God spoken to you in a time of difficulty that got your attention? What did His voice sound like to your soul?

18.3) Take a few minutes and get your journal or a piece of paper. Ask God to speak to you from His heart to yours. Write down thoughts that come into your mind from your Father God. It may be Scriptures that are brought to your memory; it could be words of a song, or just impressions that flow as you write. How did it go? What did you sense the Father saying to you? Did you hear His loving whisper of affirmation and encouragement?

DAY 19: FINDING A PRAYER PARTNER

19.1) One of the great revelations God revealed to Elijah as He spoke gently with him in the cave was the gift of a relationship with Elisha. Elijah was called to disciple Elisha and prepare him to be an instrument of God. How do you think this would have encouraged Elijah to get back into ministry?

19.2) Read 1 Kings 19:19-21 and describe the response of Elisha to the call of God, through Elijah, to follow Him? List several spiritual truths that Elisha would have learned from Elijah? Why do you think Elisha asked for a "double portion" of the Holy Spirit to fall on him when Elijah was taken up into heaven? (2 Kings 2:9).

19.3) What are the benefits of finding a prayer partner or prayer group to regularly pray with? Give examples from Scripture or from your own personal experience of the results of praying with another person or group?

DAY 20: PRAYING INTO THE PROPHECY

20.1) Malachi 4 is the last chapter in the Old Testament, and opens the doorway to the heart of God the Father found in the New Testament. As you read the 6 verses of this chapter, how is the prophet preparing God's people for His heart? Why do you think God says, "I will send you the prophet Elijah before the great and dreadful day of the LORD comes," and what will be his mission? (vs. 5-6).

20.2) As the New Testament opens we see the fiery spirit of Elijah is upon John the Baptist (John 1:19-35). How is John used to "Turn the hearts of the fathers to their children and the hearts of the children to their fathers?" How does Jesus restore us to the Father's heart of love and give us true life? (John 17:1-3).

20.3) The most important relationship we can have in life is with our Heavenly Father through His Son Jesus. How can that restored relationship heal all our other relationships in life? Meditate on Romans 8:15 for a few minutes. Why does the Father want you to know Him and call on Him in prayer as your "Abba (daddy) Father?" How can that intimate knowledge heal you and the world we live in?

❖

Jesus teaches us, through prayer, how to live in an intimate love relationship with the Father. Out of that relationship, we gain the security to live into our true identity as God's children.

❖

CLIMBING WITH
JESUS

*Prayer was a priority
for Jesus, so it should
be a priority for us, too.*

Day 21

HEARING YOUR FATHER'S VOICE

This is my Son, whom I love; with Him I am well pleased. Listen to Him!
– MATTHEW 17:5

Why did Jesus expend His energy trudging up Mount Hermon with three of His disciples? Undoubtedly, it was an experience beyond words to be present on the mountaintop with Moses and Elijah, two warriors of prayer; but I believe Jesus made the climb to hear His Father's voice and teach His disciples–and us–how to tune-in to hearing that voice.

There were times earlier in His thirty-three years that Jesus had heard the voice of His Father. When Jesus was only twelve years old and became separated from His parents, Mary and Joseph, for several days, they found Him in the temple dialoguing with the learned teachers. As a concerned mother, Mary questioned Jesus, He replied, *"Didn't you know I had to be in my Father's house?"* (Lk.2: 49). Even at age twelve, Jesus knew that being in the Father's presence was the most important place He could be.

When Jesus was baptized in the Jordan River, He prayed to His Father, who responded by ripping open the heavens and sending the Holy Spirit upon Him. This time an audible voice said, *"You are my Son, whom I love; with you I am well pleased,"* (Lk. 3:22). Jesus knew He couldn't do life, or ministry, without living into the identity of the Father's love.

Throughout the Gospels, it is evident that prayer was a priority for Jesus. After a busy day of ministry and healing in the beautiful seaside town of Capernaum, Jesus knew He needed to spend time with His Father and found a solitary place to pray. Jesus' disciples were stunned to realize that their Rabbi had removed Himself from the crowds, as powerful ministry was taking place. However, this was a teachable moment for the disciples as Jesus' identity did not hinge on satisfying the crowds, but rather in following in the steps of His Father.

It was because of His Voice that Jesus hiked 9,000 feet up Mount Hermon. It was because He wanted to be in His Father's presence. It was because He needed to be led by His Father's love, so He could complete the mission to the cross. When we **climb with Jesus**, it is vital to understand that Jesus' number one reason for prayer was to hear His Father's loving voice and to let the Father's love direct everything He did. After Jesus' supernatural encounter with His Father, Moses, and Elijah, on what is also called the Mount of Transfiguration, Jesus sets His face firmly towards the cross. He was prepared for what He had been called to accomplish.

If Jesus needed to spend time hearing the voice of His Father, how much more important is it for you and me? Remember the words of affirmation God the Father spoke at Jesus' baptism? He desires to do that for us well. Zephaniah 3:17(NLT) says, *"The Lord your God is living among you... He will rejoice over you with joyful songs."* Wow! This is what I desire in my prayer life! I need these words and songs of affirmation in my life!

If I'm truly honest, my flesh is plagued by fear and insecurity. When I drift away from having a time of prayer and intimacy with my Father due to a busy schedule or just plain laziness, my insecurities begin to control me, and I become driven by fear instead of His love. When I'm not seeking to hear my Father's voice, I'm robbed of His love, joy, and perfect peace. Jesus demonstrates that listening for the Father's loving voice was a priority for Him, and it must be a priority for us as well.

PONDER | MEDITATE | PRAY

PONDER JOHN 5:19-20

Jesus gave them this answer: "I tell you the truth, the Son can do nothing by Himself; He can do only what he sees His Father doing, because whatever the Father does the Son also does. For the Father loves the Son and shows Him all He does.

MEDITATE ON AND PRAY INTO JOHN 5:19-20

Praise God:

– for showing Himself to us through Jesus

Tell God:

– what makes you too busy for Him, give it to Him

Thank God:

– for His forgiveness

– for His love

– for His peace

Ask God:

– what do you want me to know right now?

– to show you how He cares for you

– to show you how He loves you

EXTENDED STUDY QUESTIONS: PAGE 158

A combination of fasting and prayer leads to spiritual breakthroughs.

Day 22

FAST AND PRAY FOR A BREAK-THROUGH

*Jesus, full of the Holy Spirit, left the Jordan and was led by the Spirit
into the wilderness, where for forty days He was tempted by the devil.
He ate nothing during those days, and at the end of them He was hungry.*

– LUKE 4:1-2

When someone asks me about my hobbies, I quickly respond, "Food!" I love food! That's why the subject of fasting is not an easy one for me as I love to bite into a juicy hamburger with all the fix'ns. I believe most people are like me and find fasting to be difficult. Yet Moses, Elijah, Jesus, and believers in the early church all practiced this discipline. When fasting is referenced in Scripture, it is seen as a means to bring forth a supernatural breakthrough.

In His desire to hear the voice of The Father, Jesus also fasted. A forty-day fast is recorded in Luke chapter 4. In this passage, the Holy Spirit, who was displayed at Jesus' baptism in the form of the dove, was also the Spirit that initiated the fast and permitted Satan to throw temptations at Jesus.

Jesus' fast in the wilderness was preparing Him to do battle with Satan so that He could take over as King and bring in the Kingdom of God. The forty-days of fasting and prayer empowered Jesus to bind Satan. If you remember when Satan came to Adam and Eve in the perfect garden, they had full stomachs and everything going for them as holy children of God. Yet, they gave into temptation and handed the authority of earth over to Satan. But Jesus, physically hungry yet filled with His Father's love, could overcome the temptations thrown His way.

Satan tempted Jesus, saying, *"If you are the Son of God, tell this stone to become bread,"* (vs. 4). Satan, ever crafty, was using Jesus' hunger to divert attention from his real goal of getting Jesus to renounce His spiritual identity. If Jesus did as Satan said, he'd be taking care of His own needs and not living into the will of His Father. But Jesus doesn't fall for this temptation or the others. His fasting helped him resist these three temptations, and the rest that would follow, because He had tasted the Father's love and that was enough to feed His soul.

The enemy knows that our unrealized sense of identity is our weak area. If Satan can convince us our identity is found outside of the Father's love, he has us. Therefore, Satan bombards our world with lies and temptations prompting us to consume fleshly pleasures to our heart's desire. As our culture has eaten at this table, we have found ourselves imprisoned by earthly desires that are now destroying us. Our endless lust for food, sex, money, work, hobbies, drink, drugs, independence, etc., have left us spiritually starving.

We need to rediscover the gift of fasting and pray more than ever. Fasting and prayer are key to retuning our lives to the rhythm of the Father's powerful grace. They bring us back to Jesus, our true bread of life, who fills our every longing.

Jesus shows us that, through prayer and fasting, our spirit is refreshed and fed by our Heavenly Father's love. The result is a kingdom breakthrough as seen by what follows after Jesus' victory over Satan in the desert. The Spirit was unleashed in Jesus' life to heal, bind demonic power, and boldly preach that the kingdom has come! Pray that the Spirit would empower you to engage in the gift of fasting, so you might experience a breakthrough of your own.

PONDER | MEDITATE | PRAY

PONDER MARK 9:29

This kind can only come out through prayer and fasting.

MEDITATE ON AND PRAY INTO MARK 9:29

Praise God:

– for loving us enough that we can overcome temptation

Tell God:

– about what tempts you, give it to Him

Thank God:

– for forgiving you for lusting after the things of this world

Ask God:

– for the strength to fast

– for perseverance

– that you might experience a breakthrough

❖ EXTENDED STUDY QUESTIONS: PAGES 158-159

*We need to come
to God in prayer as
a dependent child.*

Day 23

A CHILDLIKE ATTITUDE

I praise you, Father, Lord of heaven and earth, because you have hidden these things from the wise and learned and revealed them to little children....

– LUKE 10:21

In Luke 10, Jesus sends out seventy-two followers with the task of going into towns and announcing that the Kingdom of God has come in Jesus. Before they leave, He gives them a few instructions: pray, do not take any money or supplies along with you, and heal all who are sick. They followed their Rabbi's orders, and the power of God was unleashed through them–the results were staggering. They reported back to Jesus, overflowing with joy, *"Lord, even the demons submit to us in your name,"* (vs. 17).

You can imagine Jesus shouting out a big, "Yes!" He then adds, *"I saw Satan fall like lighting from heaven. I have given you authority to trample on snakes and scorpions and to overcome all the power of the enemy; nothing will harm you. However, do not rejoice that the spirits submit to you, but rejoice that your name is written in the book of life,"* (vs. 18-20). I love those verses. They reveal the authority we have been given in Christ, founded on our belief that He has written our names in Heaven's book of life.

It gets even better! As Jesus is declaring those truths, verse 21 states He was "full of joy through the Holy Spirit," the only place in the Bible where it says He was "full of joy." What brought Him over-flowing joy was declared in His prayer: *"I praise you Father, Lord of heaven and earth, because you have hidden these things from the wise and learned, and revealed them to little children..."* (vs. 21).

What brings Jesus joy is how the Father reveals Himself to "little children" or "babies." This is such a powerful point for us to grasp if we are going to climb up *Prayer Mountain* as Jesus did. We must approach God the Father as babies who are utterly dependent on their Father for everything. Jesus professed this truth as well in Matthew 18:3: *"I tell you the truth, unless you change and become like little children, you will never enter the kingdom of heaven."*

You might consider it humbling to become like a baby again. After all, our culture honors self-made giants as our models for success. But this call to become childlike should cause a hallelujah to erupt in our souls! We can stop stressing about making things happen on our own. Instead, we need only to cry out to God in dependence, knowing He is the one who runs the universe.

I'll never forget when my van wouldn't start, and I was getting frustrated. My three-year-old daughter said, "Dad, we should pray for Jesus to heal our van." I smiled, and she prayed. God listened to her child-like faith and the van started. "Okay, Lord," I thought, "You are teaching me something I missed in seminary, how to pray and live like a child trusting their Big Daddy.

God will still bring us into impossible situations like that experienced by the seventy-two in Luke 10, situations requiring us to be totally dependent on Him to provide for our needs. He longs for us to cry out to Him, trusting Him to show up and show off His power and glory in our weakness.

Today, cry out to your Daddy God, bring Him all of your impossible situations, and let Him show Himself as your Mighty Father.

PONDER | MEDITATE | PRAY

PONDER MATTHEW 18:4

Therefore, whoever humbles himself like a child is the greatest in the kingdom of heaven.

MEDITATE ON AND PRAY INTO MATTHEW 18:4

Praise God:

– for His power and glory

Tell God:

– what you depend on instead of Him, give it to Him

Thank God:

– for revealing Himself to you

– for His Joy given through the Holy Spirit

Ask God:

– to give you faith like a child

– for the ability to depend solely on Him

EXTENDED STUDY QUESTIONS: PAGE 159

Through prayer,
Jesus brings us
directly to the Father.

Day 24

HEAVEN COME DOWN

Our Father in Heaven, hallowed be your name,
your kingdom come, your will be done, on earth as it is in heaven.

– MATTHEW 6:9-10

Those closest to Jesus discovered His supernatural lifestyle came out of His secret encounters with His Father in prayer. As observant students, they appealed to their teacher to reveal how to approach the Father in prayer. Jesus willfully responds with the simple, yet profound, outline of what is historically called the "Lord's Prayer." In our journey up *Prayer Mountain,* we don't have time to discuss all the elements found in this gift from Jesus, but I would like to share three truths from this prayer that have shaped my prayer life.

Jesus' mission on earth, at its very core, was to reveal to spiritual orphans the Father's love for them. You see this immediately in the first line of His teaching on prayer, "Our Father in Heaven, hallowed be your name..." In the prayer, Jesus brings us right away to the first truth–the radical idea that we can call God "Father." This was a "no, no" in Jesus day; you would be making light of His glorious position by calling Him "daddy" or "papa." Yet this was exactly how Jesus wanted us to approach the throne, the same way He did, in intimate knowledge of a gracious, loving, good *"Abba Father"* (Mk. 14:35).

Unlike our earthly fathers, our Heavenly Father is holy, distinct from anything we have ever experienced. He lives in "unapproachable light," and His glory goes beyond the limits of our understanding. He is pure holiness, mercy, grace, justice, patience, kindness, and never-ending love. When we pray, that is the intimate, yet overwhelming, glorious Father we come to. He is more loving than the best grandfather and a billion times more powerful than all the great leaders of the nations combined.

Jesus goes on to teach us that the first thing we should request in prayer is for *"His kingdom to come, His will be done, on earth as it is in heaven."* In other words, "Bring your heavenly reign down and invade my heart with yours." Jesus' life was a reflection of this request as heaven came down and glory filled His soul. Every place He went, He brought heaven and His Father's will with Him. He preached His Father's kingdom and demonstrated it through healing the sick, casting out demons, and loving every needy person who crossed His path.

I was taught the "Lord's Prayer" at a very young age, hearing it at the family table in my home and at the Lord's Table in my church. Yet, in the years of rote repetition, I somehow missed the glorious weight of Jesus' first twenty-two words of the prayer. Praying these words from an intimate knowledge of our Abba Father will invade our hearts with heaven, and a kingdom take-over will follow. Don't miss the doorway to the Father in prayer that Jesus is showing you, and the transformation that will follow. Ask Him to reveal Himself to you. Ask Him to give you the *"Spirit of wisdom and revelation so that you will know Him better,"* (Eph. 1:17) and believe that He will answer.

PONDER | MEDITATE | PRAY

PONDER MATTHEW 6:9-10

Our Father in heaven, hallowed be your name, your kingdom come, your will be done, on earth as it is in heaven.

MEDITATE ON AND PRAY INTO MATTHEW 6:9-10

Praise God:

– for holiness, mercy, and grace

– for being just, patient, and kind

Tell God:

– that you want Him to reign in your heart

Thank God:

– for allowing you to know Him as your "daddy"

– for His kindness

– for His never ending love

Ask God:

– for the Spirit of wisdom and revelation

– to allow you to know Him better

EXTENDED STUDY QUESTIONS: PAGES 159-160

Ask for the Holy Spirit.

Day 25

COME HOLY SPIRIT FEED ME

Give us today our daily bread.

– MATTHEW 6:11

Right in the center of Jesus' teaching on how to pray is the hinge-pin petition, "Give us today our daily bread." To me, this is the most important request in the prayer, and every petition above and below it flows out of it. Though I'm sure our Good Father is very concerned with our daily physical bread, I believe in this case Jesus had something entirely different in mind. It's the second truth I've learned from this prayer.

The Greek word for "daily" is "epiousios," and this prayer is the only place in the Bible where the word is used. For years, translators have struggled with the word because it leans toward "tomorrow's" or the "next day's" bread. But how does that sound, "Give us tomorrow's bread today!" I believe it makes sense, though, when you read Jesus' teaching of the prayer in Luke 11.

Right after Jesus gives His outline on how to pray, He follows-up with a potent parable on prayer. In the parable, a man has a friend come to visit him after a long journey. Unfortunately, the man's shelves are bare, which is not a good thing in a Middle Eastern culture that places a high priority on hospitality. Desperately, the man runs over to his neighbor's house and relentlessly pounds on his door. He yells, *"Friend, lend me three loaves of bread, because a friend of mine on a journey has come to me, and I have nothing to set before him,"* (vs. 6). The neighbor is already in bed for the evening. He yells from his bedroom, *"Don't bother me…"* (vs. 7). Yet the man is desperate for the bread and keeps knocking. The text says, *"Because of the man's boldness he will get up and give him as much as he needs"* (vs. 8).

Do you see what is going on here? The needy man is asking for tomorrow's bread today. He needs the bread the family will eat in the morning right now. His need is so great, he is not afraid to be audacious in how he asks.

Jesus goes on to say that we are to keep "asking," "seeking," and "knocking for" this bread. He tells us what the bread is in verses 11-13: *"Which of you fathers, if your son asks for a fish, will give him a snake instead? ...If you then, though you are evil, know how to give good gifts to your children, how much more will your Father in heaven give the Holy Spirit to those who ask Him!"*

There is the second truth I've learned from this prayer. The mystery "bread" that we need daily, and we need to ask for audaciously, is the Holy Spirit. We need the daily filling of the Holy Spirit to know and follow Jesus. Jesus, through the Spirit, brings us into the presence of the Father where we are saturated with love and empowered to do His will.

I don't know about you, but I need tomorrow's bread today. I need a fresh filling of the Holy Spirit to bring me to my Father. Keep asking, seeking, and knocking! Your Father never sleeps; he waits eagerly to open the door and give you Heaven's Bread.

PONDER | MEDITATE | PRAY

PONDER LUKE 11:9

So I say to you: Ask and it will be given to you; seek and you will find; knock and the door will be opened to you.

MEDITATE ON AND PRAY INTO LUKE 11:9

Praise God:

– for His glorious provision of the Holy Spirit

Tell God:

– about the things that keep you from Him, give them to Him

Thank God:

– for promising to open the door when we knock

– for the gift of the Holy Spirit

Ask God:

– for your Daily Bread

– to know Him better

EXTENDED STUDY QUESTIONS: PAGE 160

❖

If we fail to forgive, our prayers are ineffective.

❖

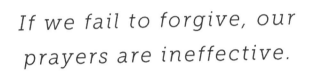

Day 26

HEALING PRAYERS OF FORGIVENESS

> *Forgive us our debts as we forgive our debtors.*
>
> – MATTHEW 6:12

Nothing stops our assent up *Prayer Mountain* like unforgiveness. I can't tell you how many times small roots of bitterness and unforgiveness have twisted around my heart and quenched the Holy Spirit. The result is a shallow prayer life that leaves my heart gasping for any type of spiritual breath. If prayer is the very air that we breathe in our relationship with the Father, unforgiveness is the stranglehold of the enemy that sucks that air right out of our lungs.

Jesus, the master instructor on prayer, teaches us how to avoid the pitfalls of unforgiveness. His instruction begins by telling us to first seek forgiveness for our own sins: *"forgive us our debts..."* (vs. 6). This is the third truth I've learned from the Lord's Prayer. Jesus takes us directly to our own need for forgiveness, which places us right before the bloody cross of Christ on Mount Moriah.

Instead of running away, as Adam and Eve did in their naked shame, we need to fall before the cross of Christ and lay all our sin down before Him. We need to let His perfect blood completely remove all our shame and guilt. His promise is that if we confess our sin to Him, *"He is faithful and just to forgive all our sin and cleanse us from all unrighteousness,"* (1 John 1:9).

Our daily prayer of confession–and trust in complete forgiveness–frees our souls to forgive others with the mercy and grace given us by Jesus. If our daily prayers for personal forgiveness are planted at the foot of the cross, then the Holy Spirit can flood our hearts with the love needed to forgive others.

This act of forgiveness applies even to our enemies. Jesus demonstrated this on the cross, crying out to all of us who killed Him, *"Father forgive them, they know not what they do,"* (Lk. 23:34). We have the power to release the same victorious words, "Father forgive..." Those words not only set us free, but they unleash the Spirit to work in those we pray for, cutting the cords in our own heart and releasing healing love in their direction.

Jesus ends His teaching on prayer in Matthew 6 by directing us back to the importance of forgiveness in verses 14-15: *"For if you forgive men when they sin against you, your heavenly Father will also forgive you. But if you do not forgive men their sins, your Father will not forgive your sins."*

I think Jesus wanted to let us chew on these heart-probing words. He wanted to underline the importance of forgiveness in our fellowship with the Father.

Today in your prayer time ask the Holy Spirit to search your heart and reveal your sins so that you may be brought to true confession. Then, out of the flood of love and forgiveness you receive from the Father through Christ, you may pour out His love and forgiveness to those around you–especially your enemies.

PONDER | MEDITATE | PRAY

PONDER PSALM 139:23-24

Search me, O God, and know my heart; test me and know my anxious thoughts. See if there is any offensive way in me, and lead me in the way everlasting.

MEDITATE ON AND PRAY INTO PSALM 139:23-24

Praise God:

– for His Holiness

– for being a God who forgives

Tell God:

– who/what you are unable to forgive, give them to Him

– about the things that make you anxious, give them to Him

Thank God:

– for the gift of forgiveness

Ask God:

– to search your heart and reveal your sins

– to forgive you of the sins He's revealed to you

– to flood your heart with His love

– for His help in forgiving others

❖ EXTENDED STUDY QUESTIONS: PAGE 161

We need to remove distractions and make our hearts a house of prayer.

Day 27

HOUSE OF PRAYER

My house will be called a house of prayer for all nations.
−MARK 11:17

I recently read a study claiming that adults spend an average of nine hours a day in front of some type of screen, and many of those hours are not work-related. We worry about how much our kids use media, but maybe we should consider our own addiction! It is not only the Western world that struggles with this issue. I have been in remote villages in Southern Africa, miles removed from a major city, where a satellite dish allows shepherd boys to peruse Facebook on their cell phones. We live in a world that is addicted to media distraction.

How would Jesus handle our media addiction if He arrived on the scene today? To be honest, I don't exactly know. But I do know He would redirect our attention to what really matters. During the last week of His earthly ministry, Jesus made a profound public demonstration that should still shake us up today.

In Mark 11, Jesus visits the temple in Jerusalem, the place where His Father is to be worshiped. Instead of worship, He finds a messy marketplace filled with noise and confusion. A righteous passion was released in Jesus; He overturned benches, tables, and anything that got in His way. In a holy fury, He bulled-over anyone who tried to sell merchandise in the House of God.

After He got everyone's attention on the Temple Mount, Jesus boldly shouted these words inspired from Isaiah 56:7: *"My house will be called a house of prayer for all nations."* This was a prophecy that declared that one day the Father would bring people from all over the world to His *"holy mountain and give them joy in His house of prayer."* However, what was going on in Jesus' day was anything but prayer that leads to joy. People were busy living for themselves, earning a buck or two for their pleasure. A relationship with God had turned into religious duty.

Jesus was about to change all that at the cross, where His mission was to dismantle an earthly temple and rebuild a spiritual temple in the hearts of all who believe in Him. Once Jesus completed that mission, **our hearts became the house of prayer**. Today, if you have accepted Jesus as your Savior, He can lead you up *Prayer Mountain* into the presence of God and fill you with *"joy unspeakable and full of glory,"* (1 Peter 1:8).

However, just like the temple in Jesus' days, our hearts have become a messy marketplace. They are like a Wal-Mart full of frantic shoppers on Black Friday. We need Jesus to come into our hearts and purge all the distractions that keep us from a having a vital relationship with our Abba Father, one that brings down heaven's joy.

Jesus modeled how to become a house of prayer. Throughout the Gospels, you will find Him leaving the crowds and heading-off to the mountains or deserts, wherever He could go to be alone with His Father. His heart became a temple where the Father came down and reigned, which revived the soul of Jesus with the fullness of heaven.

Let Jesus come into your busy life today. Ask Him to remove all the distractions, idols, and cultural noise that keep your heart from becoming a house of prayer. Let Jesus take you for a walk away from the crowds and your electronic devices. Allow Him to bring you up *the mountain*, where you will find joy in the house of prayer.

PONDER | MEDITATE | PRAY

PONDER PSALM 16:11

You have made known to me the path of life; you will fill me with joy in your presence with eternal pleasure at your right hand

MEDITATE ON AND PRAY INTO PSALM 16:11

Praise God:

– for your salvation through Him

Tell God:

– what distracts you, give it to Him

Thank God:

– for His sacrifice on the cross

Ask God:

– to remove distractions from your heart

– to make His path known to you

– to fill you with His joy unspeakable

EXTENDED STUDY QUESTIONS: PAGES 161-162

*We find security in
the Father's love.*

Day 28

ONE OF THE GREATEST PRAYERS

> *I have made you known to them, and will continue to make you known in order that the love you have for me may be in them and that I myself may be in them.*
> – JOHN 17:26

I so enjoy studying John 17, one of Jesus' most famous prayers. Jesus is in the upper room, where He's spending time with His twelve disciples before His pending death the following day. It is the last verse in this passionate prayer of Jesus that transformed my prayer life: "... *And will continue to make you known in order that the love you have for me may be in them...*" (John 17:26).

Those words from the lips of our Lord, *"The love you have for me..."* made me ask myself, "What is that love like?" I knew in my heart it was perfect in every way. We saw it break forth at Jesus' baptism and again on the Mount of Transfiguration as the Father could not hold back His feelings of love, pride, and pleasure for His only Son. This made me think about the love I have for my own kids and how I would do anything for them. Even though I'm sinful, selfish, and full of flaws, they have my heart. How much more, I thought, does the Father love me!

Jesus' mission was to make the love of the Father known to an orphan planet. At the end of the prayer He says, *"I have made you known and will continue to make you known..."* What is He making known? How the Father loves us just like the Father loves Him.

The very next day the fullness of the Father's love for us is seen as His son, Jesus, takes our place on the cross and dies for us. The Father seals the deal regarding His eternal love for us when, on the third day, He reverses the curse of sin by resurrecting His beloved Son.

The resurrection shouts the Father's love for both His Son and His adoptive sons and daughters throughout the world.

Notice the final part of verse 26: *"and that I myself may be in them."* If you believe that Christ's perfect life, death, and resurrection is for you, then Jesus will live in your heart. If that is the case, then the Father is as wildly in love with you as He is with Jesus! If Christ is in you, the Father sees only perfection, which attracts a love beyond any worldly definition.

Consequently, when the Holy Spirit unleashed the truth of Jesus' prayer into my heart, I began to constantly pray the words of Jesus: **"Father, show me the love you have for your Son is the same love you have for me."** This prayer started to become the focal part of my prayer life. It infused my mind and heart with a healing love, which brought me into a new identity as a loved son whose Father will never let him go.

My goal in my journey up *Prayer Mountain* is to know and encounter the Father's love for me. Everything I do must flow out of being secure in His arms of love. His love will affect how I live, all the other prayers I pray, and the calling the Father has on my life.

I believe Jesus has revealed to us one of the greatest, if not the greatest, prayers you will every pray. Will you join me? **Father, show me the love you have for your Son is the same love you have for me!**

PONDER | MEDITATE | PRAY

PONDER JOHN 17:26

I have made you known to them, and will continue to make you known in order that the love you have for me may be in them and that I myself may be in them.

MEDITATE ON AND PRAY INTO JOHN 17:26

Praise God:

– for His goodness

– for sending His Son that we might know Him

Tell God:

– that you want to know Him better

Thank God:

– for His love for you

Ask God:

– to help you experience the same love He has for the Son

– to fill you with His presence

❖ EXTENDED STUDY QUESTIONS: PAGE 162

We can approach the throne of grace with confidence.

Day 29

AN OPEN HEAVEN

With a loud cry, Jesus breathed His last.
– MARK 15:37

My Grandma Folkert's life was an amazing endurance race that lasted 101 years. Her journey was filled with countless hardships as well as holy moments of heaven's joy that kept her spunky spirit moving forward in faith. During her last moments on earth, just before she crossed the finish line, her eyes opened wide and her hand raised up as if to pick fruit from a tree. She brought her hand back to her mouth and appeared to bite into a piece of heavenly fruit. Her face lit up with a glow that transformed all in the room with an overwhelming peace. After her last bite she closed her eyes, breathed her last breath, and crossed the finish line into eternity. All who witnessed this moment will never forget the glorious reception of my grandmother into the arms of her Father God.

What an unforgettable scene it must have been as well for those who watched Jesus' final moments, as He completed His endurance race at the cross *"with a loud cry!"* (Mk. 15:37). In John, we read he cried out, *"It is finished!"* (19:30). This was a victory shout, not one of defeat. During the course of His perfect race, Jesus had traveled through spiritual deserts and hills filled with trials and temptations. He had hurdled the most difficult obstacles of the enemy and never took His eyes off the goal.

As the Son crossed the line, the first thing the Father did was grab hold of the temple curtain, the symbol of separation of a Holy God from unholy people, and rip it in two from top to bottom. The Father had been waiting to do this ever since Adam and Eve chose to walk away from Him in disobedience. Because of Jesus' obedience to the cross, we can once again walk freely in a love relationship with our Father.

The results of Jesus' perfect race are staggering for those who have fixed their eyes of faith on Him. In Christ's victory, we have gained complete access into the Father's presence. We don't need a priest, a pastor, or any other person to bring us before the glorious throne of God. We come in with Jesus, as Hebrews 4:14, 16 says:

"Therefore, since we have a great high priest who has gone through the heavens, Jesus the Son of God, let us hold firmly to the faith we profess...Let us then approach the throne of grace with confidence, so that we may receive mercy and find grace to help us in our time of need."

Don't miss that great news, *"Let us approach the throne of grace with confidence."* I have a Father who has opened wide the door for me. I can approach Him boldly, knowing He wants me there, He longs to hear my voice, and He wants to answer the cries of my heart. *Prayer Mountain* has been opened; the most powerful place in the universe is a prayer away. Take some time right now, put this book down, and walk into the throne room of your Father, the King of the universe.

PONDER | MEDITATE | PRAY

PONDER HEBREWS 10:19-22

Therefore, brothers and sisters, since we have confidence to enter the Most Holy Place by the blood of Jesus, by a new and living way opened up to us through the curtain, that is, his body, and since we have a great priest over the house of God, let us draw near to God with a sincere heart and with the full assurance that faith brings...

MEDITATE ON AND PRAY INTO HEBREWS 10:19-22

Praise God:

– for His Holiness

Tell God:

– what makes you feel unworthy, give it to Him

Thank God:

– for allowing you to approach Him confidently

– for His mercy & grace

Ask God:

– to speak to you and tell you what He wants you to know right now

– to show you how He cares for you

– to show you how He accepts you

– to give you release from your feelings of unworthiness

❖ EXTENDED STUDY QUESTIONS: PAGE 163

We need to learn
to wait for the
Spirit of God.

Day 30

A PRAYER COMMAND

Do not leave Jerusalem but wait for the gift my
Father promised, which you have heard me speak about.
– ACTS 1:4

It is human nature to seek instant gratification, yet there are times we must wait. We wait in lines at the store. We wait for a baby to be born. We wait for the Lord to reveal the next step in our lives. I do not know of many people who enjoy the waiting process.

I can imagine that the disciples did not enjoy their season of waiting after Jesus' resurrection. The very last command from the resurrected Jesus was to "wait!" Don't go preach, teach, organize, or heal but wait in prayer for the "gift" of the Holy Spirit that the Father promised. I can imagine the disciples were raring to tell everyone about Jesus. Waiting was not what they wanted to do.

But here is the point. It doesn't matter how revved-up and ready we may be, it must never be about us. Rather, it always must be about Him and His power working through our weakness. In Luke 24:49, Jesus says, *"stay in the city until you've been clothed with power from on high."* Jesus modeled this for thirty-three years as He waited to be annointed with the Holy Spirit. He didn't launch his public ministry until He was robed at His baptism with Heaven's power and love. If Jesus waited, how much more should you and I wait?

I can't stress enough the importance of *waiting* in our journey up *Prayer Mountain.* Waiting can be painful at times, yet this is the place our faith is forged. We must learn to trust in the faithfulness of our Father and His perfect timing.

I was trained for ministry in all the "right" academic ways and revved-up to use my newfound knowledge to change the world for Christ. Yet, God kept saying, "Wait, you're not ready." Many of my friends were busy preaching and teaching, but for various reasons doors remained closed for me.

In my final semester of theological training a discouragement weighed down my soul and I entertained the idea of throwing in the towel on ministry. One rainy January morning, I wept before the Lord: "I have had enough." In the midst of that confession, a current of God's grace flowed into our small apartment and brought a spirit of "joy unspeakable and full of glory" into my soul, (I Peter 1:8). My broken heart was "clothed with power from on High," (Luke 24:49). My life and ministry would never be the same because of the gift of the Holy Spirit from the Father on that day. After that glorious day, the Father opened doors for ministry that my mind would have never comprehended, and He continues to do so to this day.

I challenge you to take this last commandment from Jesus seriously. You may have incredible gifts and talents, even a vision from heaven, but don't move until you are filled with the Holy Spirit. The Father's timing is perfect. Learn to wait in prayer to be "clothed with power" by His Spirit. He will unleash you according to Heaven's time line, so don't be afraid to wait!

PONDER | MEDITATE | PRAY

PONDER PSALM 40:1

*I waited patiently for the LORD; He turned to me and
heard my cry.*

MEDITATE ON AND PRAY INTO PSALM 40:1

Praise God:

– for being worthy of all praise

Tell God:

– what makes it hard for you to wait, give it to Him

Thank God:

– for the gift of the Holy Spirit

– for hearing your prayers

Ask God:

– for help trusting Him

– for patience

– to speak to you

EXTENDED STUDY QUESTIONS: PAGE 163

CLIMBING WITH
JESUS

QUESTIONS FOR
EXTENDED STUDY

WEEK 5: DAYS 21-25

DAY 21: HEARING YOUR FATHER'S VOICE

21.1) Jesus takes Peter, James, and John on a steep hike up a high mountain, which I believe is Mount Hermon, to pray. As you read through this story in Matthew 17:1-13, what are the results of their time of prayer? How does this prayer encounter impact Jesus for His future ministry? What impression did it leave on the three disciples?

21.2) I state in Day 21 that I believe Jesus climbed Mount Hermon so that He could hear the Father's voice and so that His disciples would know what the Father's voice is like. Why was hearing the Father's voice so important to Jesus? Why should it be our top priority in prayer as well?

21.3) Describe what you think the Father's voice is like? How have you encountered the loving voice of your Father in your life? What keeps you from hearing His voice? Why should His voice be the most important voice you listen to? (see John 5:19-20).

DAY 22: FAST AND PRAY FOR A BREAKTHROUGH

22.1) After Jesus hears the Father's voice of affirmation and love at His baptism, the Holy Spirit leads Him to a forty day fast in the desert (Luke 4:1-14). As you ponder this passage, why do you think the Holy Spirit led Him first to the desert to fast before starting His public ministry? How do you think fasting and prayer helped Jesus overcome the attacks and temptations from Satan?

22.2) Have you ever attempted a fast from food, social media, or another type of fast? If so, share how it went. Why do you think denying yourself from food, or something else, will strengthen you spiritually? Why do you think it would be important to fill yourself up with prayer and the Word as you fast?

22.3) After Jesus descended from the Mount of Transfiguration, we read in Mark 9:14-29 that He was confronted by a man whose son was demon possessed. His disciples could not cast the demon out, yet Jesus took the boy from the father, rebuked the evil spirit, and healed the boy. When the disciples asked why they couldn't do it, Jesus responded, "This kind can only come out by prayer and fasting," (vs. 29 NKJV). Why do you think fasting is vital in spiritual warfare and defeating the enemy? Why do you think fasting and prayer prepare the way for a spiritual breakthrough? (see Luke 4:14-15).

DAY 23: A CHILDLIKE ATTITUDE

23.1) Luke 10:1-24 teaches us how to live in a dependent relationship with our God in order to be used for His glory. List several points from this text which describe a dependent lifestyle. As you look over the list, what would be the hardest one for you to follow and why?

23.2) What were some of the results of living completely dependent on Father God? How would you describe the response of the seventy-two when they returned to share their experience with Jesus? Can you share an experience from your own life where you listened to the Father's voice and stepped out in total faith? How did you feel once the faith step was completed?

*23.3) According to this passage, what brings Jesus "full joy?" Why is it so hard in our day to have the attitude of a "little child?" Why do you think Jesus says in Matthew 18:3, "**unless you change and become like little children, you will never enter the Kingdom of God"?** Why does the Father want us to come to Him in prayer like an "infant child?" Are there specific ways you can learn to become like a "little child" again in your prayer life?*

DAY 24: HEAVEN COME DOWN

24.1) The disciples observed Jesus often in prayer and could tell something special happened after He talked with His Father. From reading the Lord's Prayer, and from other accounts of His prayer life, how would you describe it? Would you agree that prayer was the most important spiritual discipline that Jesus practiced, why or why not?

24.2) *What is significant about starting your prayer out with calling God "Father?" Why was this a radical idea in Jesus day? Is it natural for you to call God "Father" or "Daddy?" Why or why not? When Jesus adds "in heaven," what truth is He seeking to get across to help us in our prayer life?*

24.3) *How would you explain the next phrase in the prayer; "Your kingdom come, your will be done, on earth as it is in heaven?" Jesus demonstrated the kingdom of heaven invading earth throughout His ministry. Give some examples from the Gospels where Jesus showed heaven invading earth. Why is prayer vital for us to bring the kingdom of heaven into our hearts? What does a life look like that has been invaded by the glory of heaven?*

DAY 25: COME HOLY SPIRIT FEED ME

25.1) *I believe this petition "give us today our daily bread" is the very heart of The Lord's Prayer. Everything above and below these words are empowered by this prayer. What are your thoughts about the word "daily" (epiousios) being a mysterious word that means "the next day's" or "tomorrow's?" Surely our Good Father cares about meeting our daily needs, but could Jesus be teaching us a deeper truth about a deeper need as described in Luke 11:1-13? What are your thoughts?*

25.2) *What truth is Jesus teaching about prayer in the story of the friend at midnight? (Lk. 11:5-8). Can you identify with the man pounding on the door saying, "I have nothing to set before him?" Share a time in your life where you felt spiritually empty or too weak to keep going? Why is the man rewarded with the bread that he needs?*

25.3) *According to Jesus, who is the gift that the Father gives to those who persistently "ask, seek, and knock?" How does the Holy Spirit fill us with the spiritual bread of heaven? Why do we need the daily gift of the Holy Spirit to live into all of the Lord's Prayer? Can you give examples from Jesus' life and the early followers of Christ where they are filled with the Holy Spirit? How can you make this prayer for "daily bread" a priority in your life?*

WEEK 6: DAYS 26-30

DAY 26: HEALING PRAYERS OF FORGIVENESS

26.1) *One of the great works of the Holy Spirit is to bring us to the river of forgiveness that flows from Jesus. Why is it essential for our prayer life to daily seek forgiveness from our Father? Give some biblical examples where people found healing through confession of their sins? Read Psalm 32 and describe how unconfessed sin effected King David? What was the outcome of his honest confession of sin? What holds you back from a honest confession of your sin? Take some time to personally confess your sins to the Father and receive His powerful love from the cross.*

26.2) *I make the statement in Day 26, "nothing halts the ascent up Prayer Mountain like unforgiveness." Why do you think "unforgiveness" will make your prayer life ineffective? Read Jesus' words after the Lord's Prayer in Matthew 6:14-15. According to Jesus, how will your Father look at you if you have an unforgiving spirit? Why is the practice of forgiving others so important to the Father?*

26.3) *Can you share a time where you held forgiveness from someone who hurt you? What were the effects of that on your spiritual life? If you can, give examples of the Holy Spirit giving you the strength to forgive someone and the impact that had on your spiritual life? Spend some time asking the Holy Spirit to reveal anyone you are bitter at that you need to forgive. Ask Him for power to release and forgive that person from all wrong.*

DAY 27: HOUSE OF PRAYER

27.1) *During the final days before Jesus goes to the cross, He makes a dramatic display of His passion for prayer by cleansing the temple. As you read Mark 11:15-19, what do you think invoked Jesus to act out His righteous anger? What does this say about Jesus' view of the importance of prayer and living in right relationship with the Father?*

27.2) *If Jesus came physically to you right now, what are the things that He would throw away that are keeping your heart from becoming a house of* prayer? What is the root cause of those distractions in your life that keep you from a passionate prayer life? What do you think the result would be if Jesus would clean out your spiritual house in order to prepare it to meet Him in prayer?

27.3) Take a moment to read Romans 12:1-2. How can your life become a "living sacrifice," a place of worship? Give examples of how Jesus and His followers modeled this "living sacrifice" lifestyle in the New Testament? According to this passage, what are the results of your life being a place of worship? What is the Father asking you right now to let go of or get rid of so that your life can become a house of prayer that brings glory to God?

DAY 28: ONE OF THE GREATEST PRAYERS

28.1) On the Thursday night before Jesus goes to the cross, He prays this heartfelt prayer to the Father in John 17. What are some of the requests that Jesus makes in the prayer? Do you think we should model our prayers after Jesus example in this prayer, why or why not?

28.2) As you study verse 26 where Jesus prays "I have made you known to them, and will continue to make you known," in what ways has Jesus made the Father known? How would you describe the Father by look-ing at Jesus? (see John 14:5-14). As the prayer goes on Jesus adds; "in order that the love you have for me." How would you explain the Father's love for the Son? Where in Scripture is that love displayed?

28.3) The prayer of John 17 closes with what I believe is one of the greatest prayers in the Bible; "in order that the love you have for me may be in them and that I myself may be in them." What would be the reason why I would say, "this is one of the greatest prayers in the Bible?" How would knowing the Father's love for you, the same love by which He loves His Son, transform your life? If Jesus now reigns in your life and you believe in the forgiveness of your sins by trusting His life, death, and resurrection, how does the Heavenly Father look at you? If you continually pray, "Father, show me the love you have for your Son is the same love you have for me," how do you think your Father will respond?

DAY 29: AN OPEN HEAVEN

29.1) We read that at the end of Christ's battle on the cross He shouted out with "a loud cry and breathed His last," (Mark 15:37). John's account adds the cry was, "It is finished," (John 19:30). How would you describe this "cry?" Was it one of pain, defeat, or victory? Why? Reflect on Mark 15:38-39. What did the "cry" do to the heart of the centurion? List all the benefits of Christ's victory cry for you?

29.2) What significance is there that the "curtain of the temple was torn in two from top to bottom?" How was the Father making a powerful declaration of His heart through this dramatic event? What significance does this have for your prayer life?

29.3) Read Hebrews 4:14-16, why can you boldly, with great confidence, climb Prayer Mountain and bring your need to Father God? Why should you have complete assurance that the Father will listen to your prayers? How should an understanding of an "Open Heaven" impact your prayer life?

DAY 30: A PRAYER COMMAND

30.1) What emotions come to mind when you hear the word "wait?" Reflect back to a period in your life where God put you in the waiting room. What was He teaching you? What do you think was going through the disciples' minds when Jesus said "Do not leave Jerusalem, but wait for the gift my Father promised?" (Acts 1:4).

30.2) In Luke 24:49 Jesus shares that they are to wait until they "have been clothed with power from on high." How would you explain this gift of clothes from the Father? Why is this "gift" the number one requirement for life and ministry? What happens when you seek to live apart from the "gift of the Father?"

30.3) Give examples from both the Bible and history of people who waited for the Holy Spirit and lived in the power of the Holy Spirit. What does a church look like that lives in the power of the Holy Spirit? Why are prayer and worship foundational for our season of waiting? (see Luke 24:50-53).

❖

Peter and John provide a powerful example of how to put the principles of prayer into practice. Their lives reflect a dependence on God, and their prayers show us how to unleash the power of the Holy Spirit to transform to the world.

❖

CLIMBING WITH
PETER
&JOHN

It is vital to be united with other believers in prayer for the movement of the Gospel.

Day 31

PRAYING WITH ONE MIND

They all joined together constantly in prayer, along with the women and Mary the mother of Jesus, and with His brothers.
– ACTS 1:14

During a season of pastoring in Western Michigan, a mighty movement of God was experienced when spiritual leaders in the community joined together in prayer. It began with a few pastors gathering on Thursday mornings, crying out to God. Sins were confessed, and prayers were raised asking God to bring revival to our hearts, churches, and communities. The Spirit swooped-in, and our small group turned into fifty-plus pastors gathering for prayer each week. In a community that was historically spiritually divided, the love of God poured out healing between generations, churches, and denominations. A spirit of unity was birthed which led to a powerful kingdom movement.

The simple model demonstrated in Acts 1:14 by Peter, James, John, and the rest of the disciples was our guide. The disciples heeded the command of Jesus in Acts 1:4 to climb *Prayer Mountain* and wait for the wind of the Holy Spirit to be unleashed from heaven. The text states, *"They joined together constantly in prayer…"* The Greek word for joined together literally means to have the same mind. In other words, the disciples developed a laser focus on Jesus, His teachings, and forgiveness at the cross. Their prayers were united around and concentrated on Christ. They understood that they needed the same power that raised Jesus from the dead to explode in their lives.

Peter, James, and John encountered the glory of Christ on the Mount of Transfiguration, and this supernatural event propelled Jesus to follow and finish the Father's will. Jesus approached the cross, a sacrificial step that would change the course of history; was raised from the dead, an insurmountable miracle; and ascended into heaven. With the disciples' rabbi returning to the Father, they knew without a doubt an invasion of glory was necessary in order for them to fulfill their call to spread the good news to all nations. So united as one, minds focused on Jesus, and crying out for the Holy Spirit, the text says they kept praying constantly. The disciples had no idea how long they would have to pray, but they stuck to it with a desperate intensity for ten days. Then the heavens ripped open, and the fire of the Holy Spirit set their hearts ablaze with the glory of God. From that moment, the church became an unstoppable force overtaking the enemy and advancing the Kingdom of God throughout the world.

Acts 1:14 remind us of the importance of finding others to connect with in prayer. Peter, James, and John honed in on this truth, which became the foundational building block of the New Testament church. The book of Acts reveals a church deliberately *Climbing Prayer Mountain* with the intent to gaze upon Christ and His glory. The results were astounding: a mighty river of the Holy Spirit flooding the world with healing, the hope of salvation, and human hearts consumed with advancing the Kingdom of God.

When I think back to those Thursday morning prayer gatherings, we really prayed! We didn't just talk amongst one another, but rather left our sins at the cross and asked for more of the Holy Spirit. We prayed with one mind. None of us could have dreamed what God would unleash in our city. I pray that the Holy Spirit will unite your heart with the hearts of others around the mind of Christ. As you cry out for His Spirit, may you come face to face with a new awakening of God's glory in the places where He has placed you.

PONDER | MEDITATE | PRAY

PONDER EPHESIANS 3:16-19

I pray that out of His glorious riches He may strengthen you with power through His Spirit in your inner being, so that Christ may dwell in your hearts through faith. And I pray that you, being rooted and established in love, may have the power, together with all the saints, to grasp how wide and long and high and deep is the love of Christ, and to know this love that surpasses knowledge–that you may be filled to the measure of all the fullness of God.

MEDITATE ON AND PRAY INTO EPHESIANS 3:16-19

Praise God:

– for His goodness and greatness

Tell God:

– what makes it difficult for you to experience His love for you

Thank God:

– for the unifying gift of the Holy Spirit

– for His peace

Ask God:

– to show you opportunities to pray with others

– to speak to you and tell you what He wants you to know right now

– to show you how He cares for you

– to show you how He loves you

EXTENDED STUDY QUESTIONS: PAGE 208

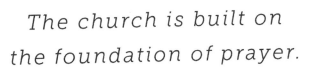

*The church is built on
the foundation of prayer.*

Day 32

EVERYTHING FLOWS OUT OF PRAYER

They devoted themselves to the apostles' teaching and to fellowship, to the breaking of bread and to prayer.

– ACTS 2:42

It is often said the three most important things needed to sustain a marriage relationship are communication, communication, and communication. When communication falters, the marriage will soon show signs of despair. The same is true of our relationship with Christ. The church is called the *Bride of Christ*, and without constant communication and time spent cultivating that relationship, emptiness, spiritual bankruptcy, and deadness will soon follow.

Peter, James, and John, three of Jesus' closest disciples, witnessed first hand His relationship with the Father. Through prayer, Jesus encountered His Father in true intimacy, and this equipped Him for day-to-day ministry. Scholars often refer to *"teaching, fellowship, breaking of bread, and prayer,"* (Acts 2:42), as the four pillars of the church. I would argue that prayer–communication with the Father–is the glue that spearheads teaching, fellowship, and communion. Together, these four components make up the purpose of individuals gathering together, whether that is in a physical church building, in a home, or being a part of ministry elsewhere.

How do you and I actually communicate with God and align our lives with teaching, fellowship, and breaking of bread? When we devote ourselves to an intimate communication with our LORD in prayer, God responds with a love, pure and real, that saturates our porous hearts. This indescribable love reveals the Word of God, *the apostles teaching*, in new and powerful ways. Prayer opens the door for the Holy Spirit to teach us the very will of God through the Word.

Prayer not only brings intimacy with our loving Father, but also *fellowship* with His children. Over the years, I have encountered an amazing revelation when I pray with others. Something in the heavenly realms happens, and a supernatural love invades one's heart. Prayer molds our hearts and minds so that we view others the way the Father views them, created in His image. I've also found that when I pray with another person–even someone I really don't know–a powerful bond is formed in the Spirit, and we become brothers and sisters through Christ's love, a *fellowshipping family.*

When prayer is a primary focus in our lives, *breaking bread* becomes a precious gift and life-giving family meal. Within the book of Acts, the *breaking of bread* refers to the Lord's Supper, and the early church readily practiced this intimate sacrament in their homes with other believers. The discipline of prayer summons the Holy Spirit to be present in the partaking of the bread and the cup. The combination of prayer and the Spirit mysteriously embodies the elements with a power that unites us, first to Christ and secondly to one another, with a heavenly bond. Participating in the breaking of bread, permeated with prayer, transforms what is often considered a traditional sacrament into a life-giving force. Communion accompanied by prayer represents the marriage feast and is a foretaste of the Wedding Supper of the Lamb when Christ returns.

The early church was a sparkling bride who discovered communication via prayer was the source of deep intimacy with Christ and others. This intimate *communication in prayer*, the *love and fellowship* that it produced, combined with *communion,* was the greatest witness to a love-longing world. These prayers of the followers of Christ increased the number of people saved (Acts 2:47). What a testimony and to think it all began with prayer!

How is your intimate communication with God? Remember, prayer is the source of everything. If communication with your Father is lacking, it will affect all the other relationships in your life. Today, make it your goal and number one passion to communicate, communicate, and communicate with your Father God through prayer.

PONDER | MEDITATE | PRAY

PONDER EPHESIANS 6:18

And pray in the Spirit on all occasions with all kinds of prayers and requests. With this in mind be alert and always keep on praying for all the saints.

MEDITATE ON AND PRAY INTO EPHESIANS 6:18

Praise God:

– for being a God who speaks to you

Tell God:

– what makes if difficult for you to hear His voice

Thank God:

– for the sacrament of communion

– for the gift of fellowship with other believers

Ask God:

– to care for others in your life

– to speak to you and tell you what He wants you to know right now

– to show you how He cares for you

– to show you how He loves you

❖ EXTENDED STUDY QUESTIONS: PAGES 208-209

*There are specific ways to
pray when persecuted.*

Day 33

PRAYER IN PERSECUTION

...Now, Lord, consider their threats and enable
your servants to speak your word with great boldness.
Stretch out your hand to heal and perform miraculous signs
and wonders through the name of your holy servant Jesus.

– ACTS 4:29-30

The journey up *Prayer Mountain* is a conscious commitment to experience intimacy, not only with the Father, but also His children. It is longing for a powerful kingdom work to take place in one's life. Yet, it is important to realize that this heartfelt desire will not go unnoticed by the enemy. Jesus and his disciples can testify–a powerful prayer life will place a target on your back and attract a few arrows from Satan.

Acts chapters 3 and 4 record Peter and John experiencing the intimacy of a love relationship–prayer communication–with God the Father. The miraculous healings and powerful preaching about the resurrected Lord Jesus demonstrate this truth as the kingdom of God breaks forth on earth. However, Satan launches a counter attack using the religious leaders of the day to carry out his plan. The result is that Peter and John are accused of disturbing the peace and end up in jail.

Once these men who *had been with Jesus* were put behind bars, the religious leaders were dumbfounded about what to do next. They hoped the display of authority, coupled with the command to stop preaching in the name of Jesus, would be enough to stop them. The men were released from jail.

I love what the disciples did next. Instead of running away in fear, Peter and John continued *Climbing Prayer Mountain* and prayed to the One who is in control of the heavens and earth. These followers of

Jesus prayed the words of David in Psalm 2, *"Why do the nations rage and the peoples plot in vain…"* The disciples knew first-hand that Jesus encountered persecution throughout His ministry, especially the events that surrounded their Rabbi's arrest and sentence to death. But still they prayed, *"Now Lord, consider their threats and enable Your servants to speak Your words with great boldness,"* (Acts 4:27a, 29).

Undoubtedly, being thrown into jail was not a pleasant experience. Yet, Peter and John claimed God's sovereign power and requested to be filled with the Holy Spirit to enable them to speak His Word with *"great boldness and perform miraculous signs and wonders in Jesus name,"* (Acts 4:24-30). Notice the Father's response: *"After they prayed, the place where they were meeting was shaken. And they were all filled with the Holy Spirit and spoke the word of God boldly,"* (vs. 31). The Father honored the disciples' prayers with another filling of the Holy Spirit, so that they could continue to live like Jesus, with boldness and supernatural power.

Acts 4:29-30 reveals Four Prayer Points that are vital for overcoming persecution:

- Fight spiritual attacks with the weapon of prayer.

- Release the battle into the hands of our Sovereign Lord.

- Pray the Scriptures, particularly the Psalms.

- Pray again for the supernatural filling of the Holy Spirit to carry out the ministry of the Gospel boldly with signs and wonders.

The next time you face the sharp arrows of the enemy in a spiritual battle, turn to the prayer in Acts 4:24-30 and put these four points into practice.

PONDER | MEDITATE | PRAY

PONDER EPHESIANS 6:10-11:

Finally be strong in the Lord and in His mighty power. Put on the full armor of God, so that you can your stand against the devil's schemes.

MEDITATE ON AND PRAY INTO EPHESIANS 6:10-11:

Praise God:

– for His strength and might

Tell God:

– about your spiritual battles, lay them at His feet

Thank God:

– for Peter and John's boldness, for their example

– for His Word

Ask God:

– to cover you with His armor

– for strength to withstand persecution

– for boldness

– to take over your battle

– for supernatural filling of the Holy Spirit

EXTENDED STUDY QUESTIONS: PAGE 209

*Prayer opens the door
to divine appointments.*

Day 34

PRAYER AND DIVINE APPOINTMENTS

About noon the following day as they were on their journey and approaching the city, Peter went up on the roof to pray.

– ACTS 10:9

I remember I was sitting comfortably at a conference, listening to a Christian leader challenge pastors to go on a vision trip to Southern Africa and see firsthand the devastating effects of HIV/Aids. I had no interest in going on such a trip, it had never even crossed my mind. Yet, I felt the prompting of the Holy Spirit to go forward. The next thing I knew, I was on my knees in prayer at the front of the stage. Weeks later, I was anxiously sitting on a plane headed to the small African country of Lesotho, a country that I hadn't even known existed. It was in Lesotho that I would have a divine appointment with missionaries Ray and Sue Haakonsen, a couple who had recently started caring for abandoned babies in their home. The ripple effect of that brief prayer at the conference forever changed the course of my life.

Obeying that still small voice and traveling to Lesotho is an inexplicable moment in my life. Since that initial trip, I continue to be involved with this ministry started by Ray and Sue Haakonsen, along with several other ministries with similar visions. Not only has this encounter from the Lord transformed my heart, but through the continued work of churches, schools, and families, countless precious babies have been rescued, adopted, and cured from the devastating effects of HIV Aids. This epic event in my life taught me the importance of listening to the Holy Spirit and His prompting to pray and wait. I can't imagine what my life would be like if I had missed this all-encompassing divine appointment.

Now, when I read about the divine appointments Peter and the rest of the disciples experienced because of prayer, I can't help but smile. In Acts 10, Peter took the steps up *Prayer Mountain*, but this time it was to a rooftop in Joppa overlooking the Mediterranean Sea. As Peter prayed, God gave him a vision. This vision didn't just happen once or twice, but three times. Yes, three times in this vision God told Peter to go ahead and eat animals that were considered unclean for Jews. As Peter struggled with the meaning of the vision, the Holy Spirit spoke to his heart. The Spirit prompted him to go downstairs and follow three men back to the house of Cornelius, a Roman Centurion. Please don't miss this part–Cornelius, who had also been praying to God, had been told to find Peter and listen to what he has to say (Acts. 10:1-23). A three-peat vision? Unclean animals? A Roman Centurion? What is this all about?

What happens next could have only been designed from heaven as Peter, a Jew, enters a Roman Gentile's home and finds it packed with his family and friends. Peter shares with them the good news of Jesus Christ, and as he teaches, the Holy Spirit floods into the home and fills the listeners with the Spirit of Jesus Christ. The whole group was saved and baptized that day. This is amazing! There was no program, no well-marketed media presentation, and no church building. It was prayer that linked Peter and Cornelius together by the Sovereign hand of God. The result was a church birthed in the city of Caesarea that would become a powerful movement in the Gentile community (Acts 10:24-48).

When the Father's children climb *Prayer Mountain* and listen to the prompting of the Holy Spirit, divine appointments will follow that will bring about God-sized movements, which will glorify His name alone. Read the book of Acts, and you will see over and over again the church grew out of prayer, which led to divine appointments where no man or ministry could take the credit. Divine appointments are waiting for you as you climb *Prayer Mountain* and listen to the prompting of the Holy Spirit. Don't be surprised who God brings to your door; open it up and follow Him. Your life will never be the same.

PONDER | MEDITATE | PRAY

PONDER ACTS 16:9-10:

During the night Paul had a vision of a man of Macedonia standing and begging him, "Come over to Macedonia and help us." After Paul had seen the vision, we got ready at once to leave for Macedonia, concluding that God had called us to preach the gospel to them.

MEDITATE ON AND PRAY INTO ACTS 16:9-10:

Praise God:

– for adopting you into His family

Tell God:

– what makes it hard to follow His voice, lay it at His feet

Thank God:

– for Divine Appointments

Ask God:

– to lead you with His Holy Spirit

– to provide you with Divine Appointments

– for a listening ear

– for an obedient spirit

❖ EXTENDED STUDY QUESTIONS: PAGES 209-210

Through prayer,
God intervenes.

Day 35

THE POWER OF A PRAYING CHURCH

> *So Peter was kept in prison, but the church*
> *was earnestly praying to God for him.*
>
> – ACTS 12:5

For members of the early church, many days were filled with hardships and heartaches. King Herod hoped to put an end to the preaching of the gospel by putting James, the brother of John, to death. Now in Acts 12, the followers face another crisis as Peter is in prison, bound-up and surrounded by a squad of soldiers. Yet the house group of believers remembered the time when Peter, James, and John ascended *Prayer Mountain* and they gathered together to pray for Peter. The reference to the word earnestly literally means to be "stretched out." I visualize people all over the floor, on their knees, continuously crying out to God to move heaven and earth for Peter, their strong and bold spiritual leader.

I absolutely love this story of prayer! Put yourself in the situation as a follower of Jesus earnestly praying for a brother falsely imprisoned. At that moment, God sends a trusted angel to awaken your friend from his sleep and escort him past guards and gates to freedom. Then, poof, the angel vanishes. Now, Peter finds himself in the middle of downtown Jerusalem and realizes he is not sleepwalking; this is reality. He hurries over to the prayer meeting at Mary's house, knocks on the door, and Rhoda answers. The young girl is so overcome with joy at Peter's arrival that she forgets to let him in. She does remember to tell the praying people that Peter is at the door, and the "pray-ers" think she is nuts. Well, Peter continues to pound, and he is finally let in. This is an amazing story! What a testimony to the power of prayer! These "pray-ers" just experienced a supernatural miracle! The prayer gatherings over the next years must have been packed! What a testimony!

I also love this next story because it demonstrates what can happen when God shows up! For some reason while pastoring in Zeeland, Michigan, God placed on the hearts of many at our church the idea of purchasing a hospital and transforming it into a ministry center for the community. So a gathering of broken people met together weekly for prayer and cried out to God concerning this idea, which was beyond them. This group of "pray-ers" lacked financial resources. They were not the "movers and shakers" in the community. In fact, many had spent much time in hospitals themselves. Fast-forward ten years after thousands of volunteer hours have been donated, countless people in the community served, and numerous ministries have called this three-story building home. Recently, I joined in via technology to celebrate the decade anniversary of City on a Hill Ministries. Praise God for this miracle birthed in prayer because a vacant hospital now hosts ministries that serve the city, county, and the world.

For me, there is no greater joy than to join with other children of God and pray for the impossible to become possible. Knowing we are powerless and must rely on an all-powerful God is the first step to seeing breakthroughs in our prayer life. We are in need of churches today that are willing to hike *Prayer Mountain* together and pray for God to do the impossible in our day. I challenge you to find a prayer meeting in your church. If there is not one, start one. Begin to "stretch out" before an almighty, all-powerful God who is waiting for you to grab His heart in prayer. Then, watch what happens when He shows up.

PONDER | MEDITATE | PRAY

PONDER LUKE 11:9

So I say to you: Ask and it will be given to you; seek and you will find; knock and the door will be opened to you.

MEDITATE ON AND PRAY INTO LUKE 11:9

Praise God:

– for being the same yesterday, today and tomorrow

Tell God:

– about the challenges you face

– about the things you need

Thank God:

– for allowing you to approach Him

Ask God:

– for the things you need

– for help overcoming your challenges

– for a group to pray with

– for more of His presence in your life

❖ **EXTENDED STUDY QUESTIONS: PAGE 210**

Through prayer, we can release our worries into the hands of God.

Day 36

THE THROWING PRAYER

Cast all your anxiety on Him because He cares for you.

– 1 PETER 5:7

I have lost count of how many groups I have chaperoned to Africa. Yet it never fails that, even with a fifty-pound limit, inevitably someone tries to fit too much stuff into a suitcase. That person ends up transferring an extra pair of shoes or jeans into their carry-on or simply leaving it at the airport! *Climbing Prayer Mountain* is about traveling with only the essentials. Spiritually speaking, lugging around fear and worry exasperates the soul and distracts us from what's important. We end up neglecting time in the presence of our loving Father. The Apostle Peter, a fellow climber, knew a little about fear and worry. He experienced what happens when you start looking down at the wave instead up to the face of Jesus; you start sinking like a brick.

After years of journeying with Jesus, Peter learned that traveling light, with eyes focused on the face of His Savior, is key! He encourages a discouraged church in midst of persecution to *"cast all your anxiety on Him because He cares for you,"* (5:7). The word cast means to throw. So Peter is literally giving permission to throw all fear, distractions, worries, and sins to Jesus. You know where Jesus puts all this stuff? The cross! The cross is the place where all our burdens, sin, and junk are hung. He carries the load, and you are free to run with His perfect heart of righteousness into the arms of a loving Father *who cares for you.* Talk about making our travels lighter!

I recently picked up one of my prayer journals from several years ago and reread a few months of entries. It wasn't an easy read as many of the hurts and struggles during a particular season of severe testing and difficulty resurfaced. Throughout this turbulent time in my life, I did a lot of throwing prayers. Page after page was filled with "God, I can't handle this! The burden is way too much, and I don't know what to do!" A number of entries simply had the one word prayer, "Help!" I was heaving heartfelt prayers, hoping the Father would catch them. During that time period, I daily cast my worries, fears, and intense anxiety upon Him.

Rereading the days and months from my journal really shed a light upon the *He cares about you* part of I Peter 5:7. I grasped how, in His time, Abba Father scooped up my prayers and answered them in supernatural ways. One of those prayers was answered right in the middle of a Wednesday night prayer meeting. A prayer warrior from Kenya was praising God for the restoration of relationships that the enemy had broken. Right then, my phone rang. Now, usually I would simply ignore the distraction, but something prompted me to check it out. On the other end was a person who I had a severed relationship with and had not talked with in months. Because of the prayer that was just lifted up to the throne room of heaven, I answered the call and quickly ran out of the room. That phone conversation led to a miraculous reconciliation that can only be explained by the Father catching my many anxious prayers, holding on to them, and answering them in His perfect time.

My journals are a living testimony to a Father who truly captures all my burdens, places them on the cross with His Son Jesus, buries them in a tomb in Jerusalem, and gives me a resurrection hope and freedom in their place. As you journey up *Prayer Mountain* today, stop at the foot of the cross and throw your burdens on that bloody tree, every last one of them. Then, turn to the trail ahead of you and take a moment to imagine the face of your loving Father who is waiting for you with outstretched arms.

PONDER | MEDITATE | PRAY

PONDER MATTHEW 11:28-29

Come to me, all you who are weary and burdened, and I will give you rest. Take my yoke upon you and learn from me, for I am gentle and humble in heart, and you will find rest for your souls. For my yoke is easy and my burden is light.

MEDITATE ON AND PRAY INTO MATTHEW 11:28-29

Praise God:

– for His steadfast love

Tell God:

– about your burdens, what makes you weary, lay them at His feet

Thank God:

– for His gentle Spirit

– for easing your burden

– for His perfect timing

Ask God:

– for humility

– to take your burdens from you

– to speak to you and tell you what He wants you to know right now

– to show you how He cares for you

– to show you how He loves you

❖ EXTENDED STUDY QUESTIONS: PAGE 211

*Whatever circumstances
you are in, you can pray.*

Day 37

FINDING PRAYER MOUNTAIN ANYWHERE

> *I, John, your brother and companion in the suffering and the kingdom and patient endurance that are ours in Jesus, was on the island of Patmos because of the word of God and the testimony of Jesus.*
> —REVELATION 1:9

Where are you as you read day thirty-seven? If you are a morning person, perhaps you're at home in your favorite chair, enjoying a cup of coffee. Maybe you're riding the train into work. What are you encountering in life? Are you in the hospital? Do you find yourself behind bars in a prison? Is today an awesome day, an awful day, or somewhere in the middle? Is your heart breaking because of life's circumstances? Take a moment and reread the verse from Revelation 1:9.

This is John, the beloved disciple who experienced the glory of Jesus on Mount Hermon with Elijah, Moses, Peter, and James. Yet here he is, years later, writing these words from prison. Apparently, the Roman authorities felt threatened by this elderly apostle. They sought to quench the holy fire and message of hope that continued to spread through the empire.

John experienced many miraculous signs and wonders as a follower of Jesus. Now he's experiencing hardships, spending his last years locked-up and separated from the flock of people he was called to lead. However, despite these circumstances, he continues to travel up the path of *Prayer Mountain*. With a heart and spirit of worship, he turns to prayer for he has learned that interceding with the Father happens anytime and anywhere, no matter how bleak or uncertain the situation. May John's words be an encouragement to you and me:

To Him who loves us and has freed us from our sins by His blood, and has made us to be a kingdom and priests to serve his God and Father–to Him be glory and power forever and ever! Amen. (Rev.1:6).

John points out three powerful revelations the Spirit brings to us when we seek Him.

- Hear that the Father loves you! His favor is on you!

- Remember Christ's blood has set you free from sin, and this means you are His sons and daughters.

- Know you reign in His Kingdom and worship as priest in His heavenly temple. Our home is in heaven.

Such powerful words bring hope to all who follow Jesus, the victorious King. But there is more. Revelation 1:10, penned by John, attests that the Father was present and spoke to John in amazing ways through prayer.

"On the Lord's Day I was in the Spirit, and I heard behind me a loud voice like a trumpet, which said: 'Write on a scroll what you see and send it to the seven churches,'" (Rev. 1:10).

The *Lord's Day* was the first day of the week, Sunday. This was the day followers of Jesus joined together to commemorate the miraculous results of the resurrection. John was *in the Spirit*, meaning the Holy Spirit through prayer and worship was leading him into the presence of God. The words written on the scroll are meant to encourage the church to overcome the enemy.

John turned his prison into a place of praise and worship, seeking the face of God. God heard John's prayers and responds. When we turn our hurting hearts to seek the Spirit of God, we too will experience words of encouragement and revelations from the Spirit. Wherever you may be, physically or spiritually, turn your spirit towards the Spirit of the resurrected King Jesus and start worshiping Him. Revelation will follow.

PONDER | MEDITATE | PRAY

PONDER JOHN 4:23-24

Yet a time is coming and has now come when the true worshipers will worship the Father in spirit and truth, for they are the kind of worshipers the Father seeks. God is spirit, and His worshipers must worship in spirit and in truth.

MEDITATE ON AND PRAY INTO JOHN 4:23-24

Praise God:

– for His love and His favor

Tell God:

– where you are, spiritually.

Thank God:

– for His love for you

– that Christ's blood has set you free

– for a heavenly home

Ask God:

– to speak to you and tell you what He wants you to know right now

– to show you His glory

– to show you how He loves you

EXTENDED STUDY QUESTIONS: PAGES 211-212

When we pray, we need to focus on who Jesus is right now.

Day 38

THE REVELATION ONE JESUS

When I saw Him, I fell at His feet as though dead.
Then He placed His right hand on me and said: 'Do not be afraid.'
– REVELATION 1:17

I thoroughly enjoy reading the book of Revelation scribed by John. The writing style is filled with dramatic images that I can picture in my mind. As a visual learner, the descriptive scenes depicted in this book strengthen my faith and give me hope for the victory that is sure to come.

When I am filled with fear, overwhelmed, or struggling in my prayer life, I often turn to Revelation 1:12-18 and soak in the visuals John saw and recorded. Be encouraged and blessed as you read about this awe-inspiring vision that describes Jesus!

- His glorious presence is ever before me as the One who understands me, for He is the *Son of Man.* (vs. 12).

- He wears a *royal robe* declaring His Sovereign reign over my life and the world. (vs. 13).

- Around His chest is a priestly *golden sash* representing my great High Priest who always prays for me. (vs. 13).

- His head and hair *glow with a brilliant snow and blinding light* that shout pure holiness and truth to speak wisdom to my needs. (vs. 14).

- His eyes *blaze with heaven's fire* refining my heart with a Father's healing love. (vs. 14).

- His feet are like bronze *glowing in a furnace* trample down my enemies as He runs to my aid.

- When He speaks, all other voices in my head are silenced by *waterfalls of His amazing grace* and mercy that rush down upon me. (vs. 15).

- He holds me close to His chest with *His righteous right hand,* which will never let me go. (vs. 16).

- He defends me before the hosts of hell with His powerful gospel that flows from His mouth like a *double-edged sword.* (vs. 16).

- He floods me with the favor of His face, which *shines with spectacular brilliance* like the rising sun (vs. 16).

As I picture the Revelation One Jesus with my spiritual eyes, I lay my life down before Him–with all my weakness, fears, sins, and needs. I wait in His presence for His perfect peace to overwhelm my stormy soul and listen for the still small voice to say, "Tim, there is no need to be afraid, just rest in who I am." When I still my spirit and allow myself to be consumed by the Revelation One Jesus, my soul is restored, and I arise in His victorious power and love to follow in His Holy Steps.

May the Revelation One Jesus described by the disciple John permeate your heart and mind, and may these visuals give you strength to keep moving upward, step by step, to encounter His presence. On this journey, allow King Jesus to walk beside you or even carry you. Fall into His arms when you are weary. Soak in His glory and victory, which He readily shares with you!

PONDER | MEDITATE | PRAY

PONDER REVELATION 1:17-18

*Do not be afraid. I am the First and the Last. I am the Living
One, I was dead, and behold I am alive forever and ever!
And I hold the keys of death and Hades.*

MEDITATE ON AND PRAY INTO REVELATION 1:17-18

Praise God:

– for His glory and might

– for His presence

Tell God:

– about what makes you feel afraid, lay it at His feet

Thank God:

– for the preview of His glory that Revelation One provides

– for walking beside you

– for understanding you

Ask God:

– to strengthen your faith

– to show you His glory

– to walk beside you and calm your fears

– to carry you through times of trouble

EXTENDED STUDY QUESTIONS: PAGE 212

❖

*Keep pursuing
the Father in prayer
until the door opens.*

❖

Day 39

AN OPEN DOOR

> *After this I looked, and there before me was a door standing open in heaven. And the voice I had first heard speaking to me like a trumpet said, 'Come up here, and I will show you what must take place after this.'*
> – REVELATION 4:1

It was a cold December morning in Colorado, and I found myself walking to a coffee shop a few miles away to finish up some writing. To be honest, I wasn't exactly in a good place, partially because of the dreary weather, but also because I was odd man out, which meant there was no car available to me. As I ambled through the snow, I cried out to Father God. I would like to say I was praising Him, but the truth is I was complaining most of the way. I asked God a lot of questions and threw out a lot of "whys." I was getting tired of waiting and wanted Him to speak.

I arrived at the coffee shop in a pessimistic mood expecting all the good seats to be filled. But to my surprise, I was wrong. The best spot, with a great view of the snow-covered mountains and an outlet to plug in my laptop, was still open. I saved this seat, got my coffee, and began to peruse my emails deleting all the unwanted advertisements. I was about to delete a message from an unknown ministry when the title caught my attention, so I opened it up. Two hours later, I was still journaling about the article I read. The words jumped from the screen right into my heart as the theme collided with prayers, dreams, scriptures I had been contemplating and even recent conversations I had had. It was as if a door to my heart had unlocked, and I could see things from a different perspective.

Journeying up *Prayer Mountain* does not guarantee life will be easy or even that we will understand everything clearly. However, eventually a door will open up to heaven, and our Father will speak the words we need to hear, at His right timing. Who knows how long John had been praying on the Island of Patmos before that glorious day when, in the Spirit, he was given the revelation of Jesus and the unfolding of His perfect plan for His people. The book of Revelation always gives me great hope to continue praying, even honest prayers of pain and struggle. Our Father can handle them and even invites them from us, His children.

Like any good father, the Heavenly Father longs to share His heart with His children. He is with us. He will never let us go. He has a perfect plan designed just for us. Like John, the Father will call you to come up and enter through heaven's open door, listen to His voice that rushes like a waterfall, see the brilliance of His glory, and know that He can replace our earthly fears with His love.

Keep coming to your Father in faith, believing that He is listening right now to the deepest needs and longing of your heart. He will open a door into His presence that will be enough for you. Even though all your "whys" may not be answered, you will find all your needs met in His presence.

That cold December day, a door was opened to me through an article I almost deleted. Incredibly, for over two hours in a coffee shop, I walked into the throne room of heaven and listened to the voice of my Father speak directly to my thirsty spirit, resulting in a supernatural peace that flowed like a life-giving river. So my friend, keep knocking on heaven's door, and eventually your Father will open it wide for you.

PONDER | MEDITATE | PRAY

PONDER REVELATION 3:7-8

*These are the words of Him who is holy and true, who holds the key of David. What He opens no one can shut, and what He shuts no one can open. I know your deeds. See, I have placed before you **an open door** that no one can shut. I know that you have little strength, yet you have kept my word and have not denied my name.*

MEDITATE ON AND PRAY INTO REVELATION 3:7-8

Praise God:

– for being Holy and True

– for His right timing

Tell God:

– about the things on your mind, lay them at His feet

Thank God:

– for sharing His heart

– for the promise of an open door

Ask God:

– to forgive you of your sins

– to fill you with His Holy Spirit

– to show you His glory

EXTENDED STUDY QUESTIONS: PAGES 212-213

The goal of prayer is to bring us into an attitude of worship.

Day 40

THE GLORY OF
THE MOUNTAIN

> *Then I heard every creature in heaven and on earth*
> *and under the earth and on the sea, and all that is in them, singing:*
> *'To Him who sits on the throne and to the Lamb be praise and honor*
> *and glory and power, forever and ever.' The four living creatures*
> *said, 'Amen,' and the elders fell down and worshiped.*
> – REVELATION 5:13-14

Worship–truly there is nothing like this gift that exposes our hearts before the throne of God and brings us up *Prayer Mountain* to encounter His glory. I remember the first time I heard *Revelation Song* sung by the praise team at a church I was pastoring. When the chorus was sung for the last time, I was totally undone before the LORD and brought to my knees:

> *Holy, holy, holy is the Lord God Almighty*
> *Who was and is and is to come*
> *With all creation I sing praise to the King of kings*
> *You are my everything, and I will adore you…*

(Jennie Lee Riddle)

Revelation Song was inspired by John's vision of the throne room of God from Revelation 4 and Ezekiel's encounter in Ezekiel 1. Whenever people or angels come before the holy presence of God, they are dropped to their knees because of the manifest presence of the greatness of God's glory. Even sinless angels can't stand in the throne room when He is being worshiped. This is the heart of *Prayer Mountain*–to be ruined by the Glory of God. Prayer and worship are incredible tools that usher us into the presence of heaven, where we are consumed and refreshed by God's weighty glory. This glory is our true home, the place where Adam and Eve lived before they fell into sin. Restoring us to this place is why Jesus came, died on a cross, and rose from the dead, so that we could return to Abba Father's pristine regal presence. Thank you, Jesus!

When the Father's children find their home in this place of abundant grace and awestruck wonder, they proclaim with King David, *"The Lord is my Shepherd, I shall not want,"* (Psalm 23:1). David learned to live in the house of the Lord, where he found all his needs abundantly satisfied. That is why he was called *"a man after God's own heart,"* (Acts 13:22). I so desire to live out of that place!

The hope in writing these daily devotionals is for us to enter into the throne room of Revelation 4 and 5, to join in with the songs of heaven, and all those who have been saved by the Lamb and the Lion of Judah. In my climb up *Prayer Mountain*, I often spend time meditating on Revelation 4 & 5 and placing myself in the dramatic scene. As I ponder the immense glory of the Lion and the Lamb on the throne, I'm prompted to join in the songs found in these verses and let the Holy Spirit bring my spirit near the King of Glory. This is where my heart belongs, this is where my soul experiences the greatest of all spiritual feasts–on His Holy Mountain.

So like Peter, James, John, the other disciples, and all the saints that have gone before you and me, keep climbing my friends. It is definitely not an easy ascent up *Prayer Mountain*; the enemy will do all he can to lure you to head back down. He realizes that once you experience intimacy with the Father through the vehicle of prayer and know heaven is your true home, he has lost you for all eternity. This encounter will ruin you in a good way, for you will know the deep love and peaceful presence of your Father God. I pray that these 40 days of ascending *Prayer Mountain* may have inspired you to keep climbing and trusting that His glory awaits you.

PONDER | MEDITATE | PRAY

PONDER REVELATION 5:13-14:

Then I heard every creature in heaven and on earth and under the earth and on the sea, and all that is in them, saying: 'To Him who sits on the throne and to the Lamb be praise and honor and glory and power, forever and ever!' The four living creatures said, 'Amen,' and the elders fell down and worshiped.

MEDITATE ON AND PRAY INTO REVELATION 5:13-14:

Praise God:

– for being our great God and King

Tell God:

– that He deserves all praise and honor and glory and power

– that you love and adore Him

Thank God:

– for His salvation

– for being the Lion and the Lamb

Ask God:

– to forgive you of your sins

– to fill you with His Holy Spirit

– to show you His glory

EXTENDED STUDY QUESTIONS: PAGES 213-214

CLIMBING WITH
PETER
&JOHN

QUESTIONS FOR
EXTENDED STUDY

WEEK 7: DAYS 31-35

DAY 31: PRAYING WITH ONE MIND

31.1) Have you every prayed with a group of people before? If so, what was it like? What value do you see in praying with others? Should praying with others be foundational for our spiritual walk, why or why not?

31.2) In Acts 1:14 we read that they "joined together constantly in prayer, along with the women and Mary the mother of Jesus and his brothers." The word "joined together" means having the same mind. Why is it important to be united in prayer around Jesus Christ? How does Jesus Christ lead the prayer meeting? What are some of the prayers you think they were praying?

31.3) You also see the word "constantly," which means perseverance or sticking to it. Why is perseverance so important in praying with others? Can you give examples of people from Scripture, or others you know, who persevered in prayer until a breakthrough came? How does praying with others in unity and perseverance bring honor and glory to God the Father? Why would the enemy want to keep the Father's children from this type of praying? Describe the Father's answer to their prayer in Acts 2?

DAY 32: EVERYTHING FLOWS OUT OF PRAYER

32.1) Acts 2:42-47 gives us a glimpse into a life-transforming church. What are the "four pillars" that unleashed this church into the world? How is prayer the "glue" that holds all the pillars together?

32.2) Why is prayer used as a tool that opens up the teaching of God's Holy Word? What would be the result of studying the Word without being bathed in prayer? How is fellowship with the Father and His family enhanced by the instrument of prayer? Can you give examples of how praying with someone knit your heart to theirs?

32.3) The "breaking of bread" or communion was practiced regularly in homes. How does prayer make this sacrament come alive with spiritual intimacy that strengthens the family of Christ? What effect did these "pillars" of the church saturated in prayer have on the family of God and on the community around them? Do you see this happening today in the spiritual community of which you are apart? If not, what do you think is lacking in order to experience what the Acts 2 church did?

DAY 33: PRAYER IN PERSECUTION

33.1) Whenever the Holy Spirit is at work, the enemy will fight back. As you read through Acts 4:1-31, what was the major charge against Peter and John? Why do you think the enemy is so afraid of "unschooled, ordinary men" like Peter and John? (vs. 13). Has there been a time you felt attacked by the enemy and what do you feel was behind it? How did you respond to the attack?

33.2) How would you say Peter and John dealt with the spiritual opposition? Consider the Four Prayer Points that are prayed in verses 24-30. Why do you think praying with the others was the first thing they did? They opened up their prayer by calling out "Sovereign Lord..." How can focusing on the complete sovereign control of the Lord give you hope in the midst of your battle?

33.3) Have you ever tried praying Scriptures during your time of spiritual warfare and, if so, did you find it helpful? Why do you think praying the Psalms would be a helpful tool in your battle? If you notice at the end of their prayer they did not ask for protection but rather for another filling of the Holy Spirit so that they could speak in "boldness" and "perform signs and wonders." What is significant about this request, and why was the Father so quick to answer this prayer? In light of the culture you are living in, do you believe this should be a pattern of prayer the church should follow today? Why or why not?

DAY 34: PRAYER AND DIVINE APPOINTMENTS

34.1) Divine appointments are birthed out of prayer. As you read Acts 10, how did Peter's prayer time open His heart to God's heart for Cornelius' household? Have you ever encountered a revelation from God in your prayer time that has changed your heart or attitude toward a person or situation in your life? If so, explain how the Holy Spirit used that encounter to change the direction of your life?

34.2) In the opening verses of chapter 10 you read about Cornelius. How would you describe his heart and his prayer life? Why do you think Father God responds in such a dramatic way to his prayers? God responds to a heart that seeks intimacy with Him. Both Peter and Cornelius are men thirsty for the presence of God. What words would you use to describe their response to God's revelation given to them through the vision and angel?

34.3) As the divine appointment takes place at Cornelius' home, how would you describe what happened? How is God glorified through this divine appointment? Can you share other divine appointments that occur in the book of Acts? The church in Acts grew out of divine appointments birthed out of prayer. In your experience of church life today, is this the model that you see followed today? Why or why not should the church depend on the divine appointments birthed in prayer for the advancement of the Gospel of Jesus Christ?

DAY 35: THE POWER OF A PRAYING CHURCH

35.1) Why did the early church need to be prayer dependent? Are there situations in your church, culture, and world that highlight the need to be prayer dependent?

35.2) In Acts 12 we read that one of the disciples, James brother of John, had been put to death by Herod. How would James' death and Peter's imprisonment motivate the church to pray? Why do you think God answered their prayers for Peter's release in such a dramatic fashion? What does this say to you about the power of groups praying together?

35.3) In verse 5, the prayer meeting was described as "earnestly praying." How do you define "earnestly?" Who is the Father placing on your heart right now that needs "earnest" desperate prayers with a group of other believers? Daily we hear of reports of Christians in other countries facing persecution and even death for their faith. Is there a group you sense God is leading you and a group of others to "earnestly" pray for in the midst of their trials? If so, make a commitment to pray for that group and other persecuted Christians.

WEEK 8: DAYS 36-40

DAY 36: THE THROWING PRAYER

36.1) What events in Peter's life led him to challenge you to "cast all your anxiety on Him for He cares for you?" (1 Peter. 5:7). As you journey up Prayer Mountain, why is it important to "travel light?" Have you experienced times where fear and worry kept you from an effective prayer time? What is the root of "anxiety?"

36.2) The word "cast" literally means to "throw." What does that look like to "throw" your "anxiety" on God? How does throwing it at the foot of the cross benefit you as you move forward in prayer? Peter adds that you are to "cast" it on Him because "He cares for you." Are there times where you felt like He did not care for you and your prayers were not answered? What did that do to your prayer life? Are there examples in the Bible where prayers were not answered and yet they kept casting their prayers up to the Father? Can you give examples of times where you have experienced the "care" of your Father?

36.3) Do you think there is value in a prayer journal, or some physical way to cast your cares to the Lord? If you have used some physical means to "cast your cares" to the LORD, describe how it went. What worry, fear, or anxiety is the Father asking for you to give Him today? Take some time to write it down in your journal or whatever way will help you to "throw it" to your Father to allow Him to take it from you.

DAY 37: FINDING PRAYER MOUNTAIN ANYWHERE

37.1) So where are you right now as you read this question? Do you believe you can turn the place or situation you are in into a "Prayer Mountain?" Revelation 1:9 says John was on the Island of Patmos as a prisoner because he followed the way of Jesus. As you read verses 1-11, how would you describe John's spirit? Can you share a time where your circumstances were difficult and yet you sensed the Lord's comfort in a profound way?

37.2) What do you think it means when John says "I was in the Spirit on the Lord's Day?" (vs. 10). What helps you get into the presence of the LORD? What hinders you from being in His presence through the Holy Spirit? Jesus makes the statement in John 4:23: "Yet a time is coming and has now come when the true worshipers will worship the Father in Spirit and truth, for they are the kind of worshipers the Father seeks." According to this verse where does true worship happen? (See John 4:1-26).

37.3) When you are in the Spirit through prayer and worship, revelation will follow. According to verse 6, what are the three truths that are revealed? How do these three truths encourage you and empower you in the midst of whatever circumstances you may be in?

DAY 38: THE REVELATION ONE JESUS

38.1) In Revelation 1:12-18, John is overwhelmed with a glorious revelation of Jesus. Why do you think John fell before Him as a dead man? (vs. 17). What are some other Scriptures where God has reveled His glorious presence to a person or a group of people? How did they react to His glory? After John falls before Jesus' feet "as though dead," what does Jesus do? What does this say about the goal of the revelation?

38.2) How would you describe the Revelation One Jesus in your own words? In John's vision of Jesus, what are the elements that speak most to your heart and why? Is there one element that the Holy Spirit is right now revealing to you that you need to focus in on for your current situation?

38.3) List several ways in which meditating on the Revelation One Jesus can enhance your prayer life? Verse 18 ends with Jesus saying, "Do not be afraid. I am the First and the Last I am the Living One; I was dead, and behold I am alive forever and ever! And I hold the keys of death and Hades." As you meditate on the Revelation One Jesus, write down some words that you hear Him speak to you through His Spirit. How do these words strengthen you as you seek to follow the Revelation One Jesus?

DAY 39: AN OPEN DOOR

39.1) What does it feel like when your prayers go unanswered? Have you gone through seasons where you felt like the doors of heaven were closed to you? What are some of the things God may be teaching you during these times? Do you think there were times John struggled with closed doors when he was a prisoner on the island of Patmos? As you survey Scripture, can you come up with others who waited a long time before a door was opened and God answered their prayer? What should their experiences teach us?

39.2) Think over the last 38 days. What have you learned from Moses, Elijah, Jesus, Peter and John that will help prepare you for an open door into the presence of Father God? Out of the truths that you have listed, which one is the Holy Spirit asking you to fervently practice to prepare your heart for an open door?

39.3) Take a few minutes and read Revelation 4. How would you describe what John saw as he walked through the open door? What did the Father want John to see as he walked through the heavenly door? Picture yourself in this heavenly scene. How would this encounter change the way you look at your present situation, your concerns about the future, and even unanswered prayer?

DAY 40: THE GLORY OF THE MOUNTAIN

40.1) The goal of the climb up Prayer Mountain is found in Revelation 4 & 5. As you read these chapters, define and describe this goal: Why is heartfelt worship the only true response to an encounter with God on Prayer Mountain? As you meditate on the five worship songs in these chapters (4:8,11; 5:9,10,12,13) what motivates you to worship God?

40.2) King David understood the goal of Prayer Mountain is to find your heart's true home saturated in loving worship toward Father God. This is why he was called "a man after God's own heart." Explain how worship and the declaration of David, "The LORD is my Shepherd I shall not want" work together? Describe how prayer and worship can bring the deepest satisfaction to your soul? What is the result of not living a life devoted to prayer and worship? How has our culture sought to preach to you a path other than climbing Prayer Mountain to bring satisfaction to your soul? How has that worked out?

40.3) *What are some benefits you have received as you have taken this forty-day journey up Prayer Mountain? What have been the spiritual battles you have encountered? Have the benefits out-weighed the battles? What are your thoughts about continuing the climb as you have finished the 40 days? Is God placing someone on your heart to encourage to take the climb with you into the presence of God?*